GOD'S
TRADEMARKS

GOD'S
TRADEMARKS

How to Determine Whether
a Message, Ministry or Strategy
Is Truly from God

GEORGE OTIS JR.

Chosen Books
A Division of Baker Book House Co
Grand Rapids, Michigan 49516

© 2000 by George Otis Jr.

Published by Chosen Books
A division of Baker Book House Company
P.O. Box 6287, Grand Rapids, MI 49516-6287

Second printing, April 2001

Printed in the United States of America

Library of Congress Cataloging-in-Publication Data

Otis, George, 1953–
    God's trademarks : how to determine whether a message, ministry or strategy is
truly from God / George Otis Jr.
        p.   cm.
    Includes bibliographical references and index.
    ISBN 0-8007-9281-5 (pbk.)
    1. Discernment of spirits. I. Title
    BV5083.O88 2000
    231.6—dc21   00-060265

For current information about all releases from Baker Book House, visit our web site:
http://www.bakerbooks.com

CONTENTS

Preface   7

1. The Need for Discernment   11
Logos, Brands and Trademarks   13
Doughnuts and False Prescriptions   15
Side Door Teachers   17
Itching Ear Audiences   20
Hearing God's Voice Takes Time   22
Heeding the Divine Traffic Signal   24

2. The Certain Sound   26
Sour Notes   27
The Articulate Communicator   28
More than a Feeling   29
Hiding in Abstraction   32
Authority Must Be Manifested   34
Learning God's Voice   38

3. The Open Book   41
Looking under the Cover   44
Let Your Yea Be Yea   47
Slippery Facts   48
Wooing versus Manipulation   49

4. The Reflected Throne   52
The Spirit of "Peacock-ism"   53
Bad Directions and Lost Signals   56
See-through Servants   60
Dealing with "the Anointing"   62

5. The Good Medicine   65
Constraining Love   67
What the Flesh Wants   70
The Plague and the Cross   72
False Prophets and Negligent Healers   76
Avoiding the Dangers of New Egypt   81

6. The Fresh Bread   83
Routines as Placeholders   84
What Is Creative?   88
Butter for the Royal Slice of Bread   91
Windbags and Wineskins   92
Interpreting Reality   96
The Divine Oven   98

7. The Fruitful Vine   99
Character and Harvest   102
Vines, Wolves and Fig Trees   105
Measuring Success   108
Unripe Fruit   110
Phantom Liberations   111

8. The Solid Rock   115
The Divine Constant   117
Fads and Fundamentals   118
Strong Foundations Take Time   121
Temporal Vessels and Living Truth   122

9. Two Roads   126
The Western Infatuation with Programs   128
Spiritual Entrepreneurs: Why I Am Afraid
   of Them   130
Seeker-Sensitive or Spirit-Sensitive?   136
From Program to Presence—and Back!   142

Notes   145
Index   151

PREFACE

I have often asked Christian audiences what an individual would need to have on hand if he or she wished to attract the company of the lovable Winnie the Pooh. Their response is both quick and sure: *Honey—and preferably two or three pots!*

Sadly, when these same audiences are asked what it takes to entreat the presence of God, their answers are far less steady. *Might it be prayer? Is it perhaps worship? Or holiness?* The equivocation is troubling in that it suggests we are better acquainted with the profile of a fictional bear than we are with the character of our heavenly Father.

This book attempts to remedy our unfamiliarity with the divine nature by highlighting seven of God's standout characteristics (or trademarks)—authority, honesty, humility, love, creativity, productivity and endurance. These characteristics tell us not only what He is like, but also what *we* will be like if we allow His presence to permeate our lives and ministries.

In recent years it has been my privilege to meet several extraordinary people who have done this. I am thinking of people like Donald John Smith, a humble Scotsman who cried out to God until revival came to the Outer Hebrides some fifty years ago—a man so filled with the presence and character of Christ that hymns and Scriptures still bubble up out of his innermost being. I am thinking as well of two African Bushmen, Jan and Piet, whose courageous four-month prayer journey up the Rift Valley in the summer of 1999 led to some of the most remarkable spiritual breakthroughs in that area in recent memory. Like many heroes, these humble men are not what one might expect. Donald John is an 85-year-old man whose intercession is still carried out in a barn on a small, storm-lashed Atlantic island. Jan and Piet are illiterate farmers whose ministry is based out of a remote village deep in the Kalahari Desert.

Although Donald John's gentle blue eyes do not see as well as they used to, he has no trouble reading God's trademarks. Jan is hunchbacked from a childhood accident, but his keen spiritual discernment gives him an almost regal demeanor. And so it goes with countless other "little people" whose absence from Western conference platforms has not prevented them from making spiritual history. They are, in the words of the apostle Paul, vivid reminders that God has chosen the weak, the lowly and the despised things of the world to shame the strong (see 1 Corinthians 1:27–29).

Personal transformation must necessarily precede community transformation, and this cannot occur apart from a revelation of God's ways and character. We must learn to see Him as He is. We cannot write our own scripts. And we must also learn to see Him *where* He is, realizing that this will not always be in places or in people we might expect.

Each section of this book presents a specific emphasis. And since emphases by their very nature are narrow and focused, readers looking for balance should plan to absorb the entire work. Where I have been critical, I have tried to focus on behavior rather than people. When individuals fall short, it is often because they are immature, not because they are evil. Few of us are what we were five years ago.

God's character is marvelous, a wonder to behold. I trust you will enjoy examining His trademarks as much as I have.

George Otis Jr.
Lynnwood, Washington

ONE

THE NEED
FOR DISCERNMENT

*The idolatrous heart assumes that God is other than He is—
in itself a monstrous sin—and substitutes for the true God
one made after its own likeness.*[1]

A. W. Tozer

Rarely a week goes by that I am not tempted to disengage
from this world and pursue a simpler lifestyle. Since I am a
perennial frequent flier, my particular fantasy involves ex-
changing the cacophony of overburdened airline terminals for
a serene writer's cottage by the sea. Instead of muscling lug-
gage into congested overhead bins, I indulge in a good book
or a late-night Scrabble game by a roaring fire.

Unfortunately the dreamlike images are short-lived. In reality my life, and the lives of most people, are an unending

marathon of decision-making, a target for option-wielding travel agents, persistent advertisers and datebook-carrying conference organizers. While some will doubtless insist the solution lies in making select career or lifestyle adjustments, I am convinced the mounting pressure and confusion are inherent to the hour in which we live.

According to British author Os Guinness, this pressure derives from the proliferation of choice and change that is rapidly multiplying the number of options available to us. Left unchecked by a clear perception of divine calling, which Guinness calls the "bull's-eye at the center of the widening concentric circles that are life's possibilities," this condition leads quickly to "a sense of fragmentation, saturation, and overload."[2]

In fact, the quandaries facing active and concerned Christians have never been so numerous or pronounced. Even the process of selecting a church home has devolved into a dance of astonishing complexity. Instead of simply considering a fellowship's proximity to hearth and home, we must now contend with a lengthy checklist of preferences: Do we prefer Catholic or evangelical? charismatic or mainline? homogenous or multicultural? traditional or "seeker-sensitive"? And these questions are just the beginning.

If we are looking for additional or specialized teaching, we are forced to sort through stacks of conference brochures, television promos and magazine ads emblazoned with more speaker photos than a high school yearbook. Having finally made our choice, we arrive at the seminar only to confront a daunting array of workshop options and book tables piled higher than a king's ransom. Bound in visually enticing covers, these pulp and print missives shout for our attention like a room full of painted ladies: "Pick me!" "Buy me!" "Read me!" Unfortunately they present themselves with only the sparest credentials, leaving us, once again, to reach our own conclusions.

Confining ourselves to home brings little relief. Some of the most daunting challenges to our discernment walk in with the daily mail. They arrive in the form of letters entreating us to help fill the stomachs of hungry refugees, return prayer to public schools, provide Bibles for prisoners or fund a missionary venture in Nicaragua. Others ask us to volunteer at the church youth camp or commission our home as a Lighthouse of Prayer. The causes are as noble as they are numerous. The individuals and institutions issuing the appeals are worthy, or seemingly so. The challenge is in deciding where our resources will go. To what and to whom do we give ourselves?

It is not an easy task. We are living in Christianity's most entrepreneurial season. Revivals and outpourings are being marketed with the same aplomb as trade shows and conventions. Slickly packaged conferences and teaching products pressure us to "upgrade" to the latest version. "Surefire" programs are as common as Internet startups. And if this were not confusing enough, each new idea and initiative is championed as the offspring of the divine mind and will.

This tendency to invoke God's name is understandable, but it also raises an important question: How do we differentiate the quality imitator from the real thing?

Logos, Brands and Trademarks

What comes to mind when you hear the word *trademark?* Do you picture the Nike swoosh? The stylized red waves of Coca-Cola? The roaring lion of MGM? The golden arches of McDonald's? Maybe you see the bovine splotches of Gateway Computer or the big black ears and endearing smile of Mickey Mouse. Whatever images are conjured, one thing is certain: They have been imprinted on your mind through relentless advertising. They are the product of cold calculation.

Trademarks and brands serve two purposes. First and most obvious, *they identify a product's origin or ownership*. Almost daily we use products whose names and logos reveal where they were created or where they may be obtained. In other situations an item's special markings can help us sort out to whom it belongs. (This is the idea behind cattle branding.)

The second function of a brand or trademark is to *highlight values and distinctiveness*. Not all products are the same. Some are produced with quality parts and great care. Others stand out because they possess a unique feature or ingredient. By drawing attention to these differences, a trademark helps to facilitate consumer bonding.

Despite the claims of the Pepsi Corporation (the people who brought us the "Joy of Cola") that consumers can easily distinguish their product from Coke, they have no intention of shipping plain aluminum cans. They want their red, white and blue trademark to continue capturing shoppers' attention. They also want to ensure that the grocer forwards sales receipts to the proper owner. Likewise Texaco is not about to suggest that you can trust your car to whatever gasoline or automotive mechanic happens to be handy. Nor, if leading chip-maker Intel has anything to say about it, will you ever unpack a new computer emblazoned with the generic phrase *Quality Processor Inside*.

Trademarks have become transmitters of messages dealing with genuineness and quality. They are a means of inspiring customer confidence, assuring us that we are getting the real thing. Often they are reinforced with slogans like:

"With a name like *Smuckers*, it has to be good."
"It's not just underwear, it's *Hanes*."
"*Hallmark*, when you care enough to send the very best."

It is possible to buy fifteen-dollar watches from street hawkers that bear the Rolex trademark. But you can be sure the

50.00
50.00
100.00
820.00

268
351.10

640 = 5×128 = 640-62
-/2

1785

Rolex company is not happy with the fact that these watches have Timex components in them. The same might be said of French fashion designer Louis Vuitton, whose wallets and handbags are routinely counterfeited and sold through online auction houses like eBay.

If counterfeit items are synonymous with substandard components and care, the same may not necessarily be said of products we have come to identify as "generics." These unadorned and often deeply discounted items range from denim jeans and auto parts to cornflakes and birth control pills. And while it is true that generics often offer comparable quality to brand names at a cheaper price, there is one significant catch: This is not *always* so. Sometimes the quality of the generic item is decidedly inferior. And since the manufacturers of these products do not advertise or otherwise identify themselves, it is difficult to know exactly who you are dealing with. The bottom line is that generics are a gamble. You can save big; you can also lose out.

Doughnuts and False Prescriptions

The spiritual arena has its share of counterfeits and generics. The former use God's name to disguise evil motives and messages (see Matthew 7:15–23), while the latter try to equate flesh-inspired initiatives with those born of the Spirit (see Romans 2:28–29; 3:20; 8:8; Galatians 6:12–15). If spiritual generics are not evil, they are certainly immature.

Discernment requires perspective. It is not how things look that determines their value but how we look at them. The man who has undergone triple-bypass heart surgery is no longer seduced by triple-thick eggnog or chocolate silk decadence. He has learned the hard way that tasty foods are not always nourishing. French crullers and cream puffs may once have provided a feast for the senses, but they are now more threatening than a nest of vipers.

So it is with much of today's sensually oriented "ministry." Nattily attired televangelists, slickly choreographed concerts and superlative-laced appeal letters are not intrinsically evil, but neither should we mistake their incandescence for divine light. As we shall see in chapter 6, "great swelling words" (2 Peter 2:18, KJV; see Jude 16) tend toward spiritual vanity (emptiness) rather than spiritual health. They do not kill instantly, but their lack of godly nourishment eventually robs us of the strength and discernment we need to ward off more serious deception.

Strange as it may sound, we can even be harmed by messages and ministries that are genuine products of heaven. This happens when we imbibe a good word or work at the wrong time or at an excessive dosage. The appropriateness of a treatment must be based on our present condition. Good medicine in the wrong body can become deadly poison. This is why medical experts warn us against taking a medication that was prescribed for someone else. It is also why we should be wary of Christian ministers whose "one-revelation-fits-all" prescriptions are a form of spiritual malpractice.

Western Christians are vulnerable on two counts. First, we are surrounded by an ever-increasing number of false prophets and religious manipulators. These people are highly skilled at masking their true intentions, and will, if not exposed on some evening news magazine, take us for a long and painful ride. Second, as I indicated earlier, we are subjected to a cacophony of well-intentioned but otherwise misguided messages and pleas. We are encouraged to purchase "cutting-edge" books only to discover they are yesterday's dinner. We are entreated to contribute to "breakthrough" initiatives only to learn they have life spans rivaling those of the common housefly.

On the one hand, we want to avoid being hurt or deceived; on the other, we want to avoid wasting valuable time and money. We know suspect people and ideas are in circulation. What we lack is a means of quickly and accurately evaluating their spiritual credentials.

Side Door Teachers

The second epistle of Peter warns against latter-day false teachers who "will secretly introduce destructive heresies" (2 Peter 2:1). The word *secretly* (the King James uses *privily*) is chosen carefully here, appearing in no other New Testament passage. It is drawn from the Greek word *pareisago*, meaning "to lead in sideways." The clear suggestion is that false teachers do not bring their message in by the front entrance. Like troubled teens trying to sneak undesirable friends into their parents' houses, they have something to hide. Needing a way to bypass the sentries of truth and conscience, they look for unlocked basement doors.

Unfortunately these moral cat burglars are very good at what they do. They are at once stealthy and charismatic, and "*many* shall follow their pernicious ways" (2 Peter 2:2, KJV, emphasis added). This observation is repeated in Matthew 24:11, where we are told that in the last days "*many* false prophets shall rise, and shall deceive *many*" (KJV, emphasis added). The sobering results are summarized in Matthew 7:21–23:

> "Not everyone who says to me, 'Lord, Lord,' will enter the kingdom of heaven, but only he who does the will of my Father who is in heaven. *Many* will say to me on that day, 'Lord, Lord, did we not prophesy in your name, and in your name drive out demons and perform many miracles?' Then I will tell them plainly, 'I never knew you. Away from me, you evildoers!'"
>
> emphasis added

What chilling words to flow out of the mouth of God! And what an unwelcome surprise! Clearly these prophetic, miracle-working exorcists think they are in good standing with the Almighty. They certainly approach Him on familiar terms. In the end, however, they are dismissed. It no longer matters that they have cast out demons or attended church faithfully. No mercy is extended because their philosophy of ministry was shared by many others. They have walked and ministered in deception, and the consequences are eternal.

How are we to avoid joining this tragic throng? Peter warns that in the last days false teachers will endeavor to "exploit" us with deceptive words (2 Peter 2:3). In the original Greek this exploitation involves being "trafficked as merchandise." It puts us in the same predicament as the college athlete whose services are coveted by professional sports teams. We are sweet-talked by false teachers whose real concern is to build their franchise. We are exploited "with stories they have made up" (verse 3). We are told what we want to hear.

Fortunately the Bible offers a profile of these deceptive teachers so we can avoid their snares. The most complete version is found in 2 Peter 2:

1. *False teachers despise authority* (verse 10). As self-willed, self-exalting operators, they neither want nor practice any form of accountability. Their ministry boards are stacked with relatives and sycophants whose sole responsibility is to facilitate their imperial ambitions. Outsiders who question their motives, doctrine or methodologies are subjected to a barrage of self-righteous fury.

2. *False teachers are arrogant and presumptuous* (verse 10). Not only do they use God's name to advance self-inspired plans and philosophies; they make an artful habit of claiming spiritual authority they do not possess. This latter tendency is particularly evident among audience-conscious prayer warriors who "slander celestial beings" and "blaspheme in matters they do not understand" (verses 10, 12).

3. *False teachers revel in pleasure* (verse 13). Having become addicted to self-indulgence, religious charlatans develop what the apostle Peter called "eyes full of adultery" (verse 14). No longer satisfied with their present call-

ing and comforts, they embark on an obsessive quest to steal their neighbors' possessions—most notably money, "sheep" and prestige. In the end, truth is the chief victim of this libidinous lifestyle.

4. *False teachers are experts in greed* (verse 14). They have learned how to milk trusting congregations and mailing lists for all they are worth. Their actions flow out of covetous hearts that have been trained through regular exercise. Like the young Levite from Bethlehem in Judah, they are willing to sell their priestly services for money and merchandise (see Judges 17:10–11). Like Balaam they love "the wages of wickedness" (2 Peter 2:15).

5. *False teachers seduce the unstable* (verse 14). The favored quarry of these spiritual hustlers are seekers and newborn Christians "who are just escaping from those who live in error" (verse 18). They stalk such persons for the same reason a sexual predator targets a love-starved child or jilted spouse—vulnerability. Recognizing an emotional void, false teachers position themselves to "allure through the lusts of the flesh" (verse 18, KJV).

6. *False teachers are wells without water* (verse 17). They enjoy being sought out by thirsty people but they offer no spiritual depth or nourishment. They attract crowds with "great swelling words of vanity" (verse 18, KJV)— big talk energized by charisma rather than godly content. Their "gift of convocation" generates a multitude of followers but few, if any, mature disciples.

In the end false teachers are dangerous precisely because they are *false*. "They promise [their followers] freedom, while they themselves are slaves of depravity" (verse 19). Their behavior is analogous to a skeletal street junkie passing a syringe to a runaway teen and saying, "Trust me, in a few seconds all your worries will go away." They are the herpes-infected lady-killer who coos to the starry-eyed virgin, "Let me teach you what living is all about." They are the debt-laden relative who unceasingly extols the "freedom" of credit cards.

What is it that makes these messengers, and their messages, so persuasive?

Itching Ear Audiences

Whenever a prominent pastor, televangelist or ministry leader is exposed in scandal, our first question tends to be, How could this have happened? By "this" we mean the bad judgment, the fall from grace, the broken lives. While the question is understandable in light of the immediate pain and furor, I believe it masks an even more important question: *How did someone pursuing a secret life of sin and walking out of sync with God's Holy Spirit still manage to attract us as ardent followers and supporters?* Is not the failed discernment of the many a bigger spiritual concern and headline than the sins of the one?

Paul, in his second letter to Timothy, warned that in the last days people will be "lovers of pleasure rather than lovers of God" (2 Timothy 3:4). They will cultivate "a form of godliness" but will also deny its true power (2 Timothy 3:5). While acknowledging that "evil men and impostors will go from bad to worse" (verse 13), the apostle offered no comfort to their self-centered followers.

The time is coming, he said, when religious people "will not put up with sound doctrine" (2 Timothy 4:3). Instead they will surround themselves with "a great number of teachers" prepared "to say what their itching ears want to hear" (v. 3). Eventually, Paul told Timothy, they will stop listening to truth altogether (v. 4).

The King James Version uses the word *heap* to describe the process of accumulating teachers who will comfort and captivate. The term is derived from the Greek *episorcuo* and means "to accumulate in piles." It highlights a practice that is both greedy and dangerously indiscriminate. Those who pursue it are so eager to be entertained that they often make no real effort to assess their teachers' spiritual credentials or personal integrity.

One pastor, anguished over the spiritual recalcitrance and narcissism of certain parishioners, put his concerns to verse:

> Here they come,
> my nonchalants,
> my lazy daisies,
> their dainty perfume
> disturbing the room
> the succulent smell
> seductive as hell.
>
> Here they are
> my pampered flamboyants,
> status spoiled, who bring
> with exquisite zing
> their souls spick and span
> protected by Ban,
>
> Their hearts young and gay
> decked in handsome cliché,
> exchanging at my call
> with no effort at all
> worship for whispering
> God for gossiping
> theology for television.
>
> Baptized in the smell
> of classic Chanel
> I promote their nod
> to a jaunty God
> Who, they are sure,
> is a sparkling gem
> superbly right for them.

> There they go
> my in-crowd
> my soft-skinned crowd,
> my suntanned, so-so
> elegant, swellegant,
> natty, delectable,
> suave, cool, adorable,
> DAMNED![3]

After the apostle Paul warned Timothy about just such people, he added, "But you, keep your head in all situations" (2 Timothy 4:5). The New King James Version renders the phrase: "But you be watchful in all things." False teachers and messages thrive in the arena of the flesh. This is why we must learn to see with spiritual eyes. If we do not look beyond the flesh, we will be seduced by the flesh.

Hearing God's Voice Takes Time

If we are to identify spiritual generics, counterfeits and false prescriptions, we must first learn to recognize the real thing. We need the ability to discern God's voice regardless of whether it is delivered via a ministry newsletter, a shiny new book, a Christian music album or a pulpit preacher.

Most people are deceived because they refuse to adopt a spiritual viewpoint. It takes time to learn the principles and protocols of the spiritual dimension, and many Christians lack the necessary patience. Those who persevere, however, develop valuable spiritual sense organs—organs the Bible refers to as "eyes that see" and "ears that hear" (Deuteronomy 29:4).

It is these spiritual organs that allow us to discern the voice (or characteristics) of our Shepherd. They function like sophisticated modern receivers—televisions, radios, telephones, radar and sonar, to name a few—that are capable of "reading" otherwise silent signals. The *ping* of a downed aircraft's black box may be echoing through the ocean depths, but this means nothing if investigators are not outfitted with the right equipment to detect it. The same could be said of expensive satellites that transmit radio signals back from the outer reaches of the solar system.

These same spiritual organs allow us to distinguish the voice of our Shepherd from the voice of a stranger. In John 10:5 the term *stranger* means "belonging to another." It is distinct from *xenos,* the normal Greek word for *foreigner.* When Jesus said of His disciples, "They will never follow a stranger" (John 10:5), He spoke not of somebody His disciples had not seen before (a foreigner), but about someone who belonged to another (a misfit).

Armed with this understanding, we might rephrase John 10:3–5 as follows:

> "My true followers, having spent quality time with Me, have grown accustomed to My appearance and voice. This is why they are never confused or hesitant to follow Me. It is also the reason they are unresponsive to entreaties brought by representatives of other masters."

It has been said that the process of getting to know another person, or the process of falling in love, depends to a considerable extent on listening to what the other person says, and asking questions to find out what he or she feels and thinks. Since Christianity is, in essence, a relationship, one would think this type of interpersonal exploration and discovery would be a natural pursuit of Christians in quest of eternal love. In many cases, unfortunately, it is not.

Many professing Christians today seem more interested in immortality than in relationship. Their discussions center on eternal life rather than eternal love. But what is eternal life without an eternal love? C. S. Lewis, referring to immortality, wrote, "For my own part I have never seen how a preoccupation with that subject at the onset could fail to corrupt the whole thing."[4]

An intimate, personal relationship, if we are to grant these words their due, can be experienced only like with like. This is why we will never see a human being experiencing intimate fellowship with a water buffalo. If we fail to take advantage of the unique Spirit-to-spirit channel God has set up for deep communion, He will forever remain a mystery to us. His still, small voice will be drowned out by the religious hustle, the run-of-the mill sermon, the good advice that was never meant for us. Not knowing the Way, we will end up like the holiday-maker trapped in a house of mirrors. What begins as great fun soon turns to frustration, and eventually full-fledged panic. Unable to distinguish exits from reflections, we bump into ourselves at every turn.

This scenario is tragic not only because of its ending but because it is so common—and so avoidable. God has given us everything we need for success—*if* we slow down and listen, *if* we settle back and observe. Our first act should be to savor the extraordinary prospect of courting, and being courted by, the Creator of the universe.[5]

> Then God said, "Let us make a man—someone like ourselves, to be the master of all life upon the earth and in the skies and in the seas." So God made man like his Maker. Like God did God make man. . . .
>
> Genesis 1:26–27, TLB

Heeding the Divine Traffic Signal

We end this chapter with many of the same questions we started with: How do we differentiate the quality imitator from the real thing? What qualities or characteristics validate divine origin and ownership? What do we do if we cannot recognize God's trademarks?

While the first of these inquiries has already been addressed, at least in part, the second awaits further examination. It is an important question; indeed, the answer consumes the lion's share of our remaining chapters. The core of this material consists of a thoughtful review of seven divine trademarks—a roster that in no way implies I have identified *all* of God's expedient characteristics. What I do contend is that these seven trademarks will always be present in any true product of heaven.

As to the third question, the best advice I can offer is that we should respond to moral trademarks as if they were colored lights on a traffic signal. If and when we recognize a label as God's own, we have a green light to follow whatever message or ministry carries it. The apostle Paul admonished, "The things which you learned and received and heard and saw in me, these do . . ." (Philippians 4:9, NKJV). If, on the other hand, we have not been able to discern a ministry's trademarks, then we need to operate with a yellow light of caution. We do not reject a ministry on the basis of hearsay or rumor, but neither should we be too quick to endorse outward trappings of success. Of course, if a messenger clearly belongs to another, we need to acknowledge the red light flashing in our spirit by coming to a rapid and complete stop.

Finally, God's willingness to interact with us is always predicated on the cleanness of our hearts. We cannot cut moral corners and at the same time expect divine favor. King David learned this the hard way, and his understanding on the matter is set forth in the unvarnished language of Psalm 66:18: "If I regard iniquity in my heart, the Lord will not hear" (NKJV).

With religious entrepreneurs tempting us with an ever-growing, ever more dazzling list of programs, products and possibilities, spiritual discernment has become a critical skill. The quickening pace of life only complicates matters, demanding that our judgments be swift as well as sound. We can succeed, but only if we learn to linger in the Master's presence.

TWO

The Certain Sound

Have not I written to thee excellent things in counsels and knowledge, that I might make thee know the certainty of the words of truth . . . ?

Proverbs 22:20–21, KJV

Just under two thousand years ago a remarkable event took place in the city of Jerusalem. Although the scriptural record is short on details, it is clear that the incident occurred at a gathering of the apostles. The intended purpose of this assembly was likely prayer or fellowship; they were, we are told, in "one accord" (Acts 2:1, KJV). Even so, what happened there could hardly have been predicted, let alone fully prepared for. This modest group of fishermen-cum-apostles was overwhelmed, apparently without warning, by a force so ancient and otherworldly that it reduced all prior plans and expectations to insignificance. And it began, the record states, when "there came a sound from heaven . . ." (Acts 2:2, KJV).

Scripture goes on to describe this heavenly sound as something like a "rushing mighty wind." It was the *ruach* or Spirit of God, and it doubtless set the apostles' hair at military attention. Like Job before them, they might well have declared:

> "At this my heart pounds
> and leaps from its place.
> Listen! Listen to the roar of his voice,
> to the rumbling that comes from his mouth."
>
> Job 37:1–2

How different is this sound from what we are accustomed to hearing in church today? How long has it been since the awesome voice of the Almighty has caused our hearts to pound within us? We may long to hear a "rushing mighty wind," but we are more likely to get a blast of religious hot air.

Sour Notes

In his first epistle to the Corinthians, Paul compared spiritual communication to the sounds produced by various musical instruments. "How," he asked, "will anyone know what tune is being played unless there is a distinction in the notes" (14:7)? Similarly, if a trumpet blows an uncertain sound, "who will get ready for battle" (verse 8)?

Christians are often confused by the discordant sounds emanating from religious authors, ministers and musicians. They appreciate the talent but not the mixed messages. In many cases God's original score has been improvised on (see Amos 6:5) beyond recognition. They can no longer tell who is speaking or precisely what is being said.

That we find sour notes unpleasant and distracting is not bad. It suggests that an unconscious discernment is occurring, a recognition that something is out of place. It is a reminder that God's music is written on our hearts at birth, and even if we never learn to play it, we can at least detect a deviant melody.

Moreover, this discernment improves with practice. It matures in proportion to the time we spend listening to the real thing. Eventually our ears are able to detect not only God's voice, but the tone of His voice.

God's speech has a certain sound, and this is His first trademark. It conveys both *specificity* and *authority*—characteristics we will now examine in detail.

The Articulate Communicator

Many Old Testament prophets prefaced their remarks with the phrase *And the word of the Lord came to me, saying*.... They wanted it known that they had received an articulate message from the living God. He had spoken to them without stuttering or equivocation. His intentions were neither vague nor arbitrary.

This is God's way. He always homes in on specific issues. When He speaks to a matter, we are not left to wonder what He is thinking. The wealthy young ruler discovered this when he endeavored to access Jesus' inner circle. For the first time in his life his résumé meant nothing. His religious pretension was cut down by four simple words: "One thing you lack ..." (Mark 10:21).

The Word of the Lord is a razor, not a butter knife. Like all sharp instruments, it is intended to cut and penetrate, to divide and discern. If we let it do its work, it will strip away our illusions and help us order our thoughts. It will take us beneath the flotsam and jetsam of life and point us to the basement of reality.

God has not placed us in a cosmic game show where His will can be discerned only through chance, guesswork or experimentation. If He is displeased with us, He will tell us why. If we have gone off-course, He will tell us where. He is a lover, not a sadist.

Ambiguity can be annoying, especially when it is associated with power and expectation. Imagine, for example, having the following conversation with an agent of the Internal Revenue Service:

"Hello, Mr. Chang. I am phoning to inform you that your tax bill will be considerably higher next year."

"Really? How much higher?"

"We haven't been able to determine that yet."

"Well, how will you reach a final figure?"

"Unfortunately we're not quite sure."

"Can you at least tell me when I need to file my return?"

"No, we haven't decided."

"What method of payment will you accept?"

"I'm sorry, Mr. Chang, we don't really know that either."

Any message that is truly of God will come to the point; it will lead us to a conclusion. If what we are hearing is repetitive, rambling, ambiguous, confused or generalized, it is probably time to head in another direction.

More than a Feeling

In the absence of specific or intimate communication, people will eventually come to see God as an impersonal concept rather than a personality. To religious traditionalists He tends to devolve into a theological notion; to spiritual mystics He retreats into a shadowy sense or presence. This situation, as A. W. Tozer wrote in *The Knowledge of the Holy*, has serious ramifications, not only for us as individuals but also for the Church at large:

The most portentous fact about any man is not what he at a given time may say or do, but what he in his deep heart conceives God to be like. We tend by a secret law of the soul to move toward our mental image of God. That our idea of God correspond as nearly as possible to the true being of God is of immense importance to us. Compared with our actual thoughts about Him, our creedal statements are of little consequence. . . . A right conception of God is basic not only to systematic theology but to practical Christian living as well. It is to worship what the foundation is to the temple. . . . Before the Christian church goes into eclipse anywhere, there must first be a corruption of her simple basic theology. She simply gets a wrong answer to the question, "What is God like?" and goes on from there.[1]

Before we can even inquire into God's likeness and character, however, we must confront another, more fundamental question: Does God *want* us to know Him? If He is at all resistant to discovery—a position advocated by certain Reformers—there is little we can do.

Happily the evidence seems to weigh against those early Reformers. If we are to take Scripture at face value, it is clear that God not only wants us to know Him, but He places top priority on it.

"I desire mercy and not sacrifice,
And the knowledge of God more than burnt offerings."

Hosea 6:6, NKJV

Thus says the LORD:
"Let not the wise man glory in his wisdom,
Let not the mighty man glory in his might,
Nor let the rich man glory in his riches;
But let him who glories glory in this,
That he understands and knows Me. . . ."

Jeremiah 9:23–24, NKJV

Rather than remain mysterious and aloof, history records that Jehovah has gone to great lengths in order to reveal Himself to mankind. As He once asked the Israelites, through Moses:

> Has any god ever tried to take for himself one nation out of another nation, by testings, by miraculous signs and wonders, by war, by a mighty hand and an outstretched arm, or by great and awesome deeds, like all the things the LORD your God did for you in Egypt before your very eyes? You were shown these things so that you might know that the LORD is God; besides him there is no other.
>
> Deuteronomy 4:34–35

Nor are signs and wonders God's only means of communication. He has also reached out at various times through the wonders of nature, through godly prophets, animal sacrifices, angelic messengers and holy Scripture—the latter being a particularly explicit disclosure. My Bible has 1,635 pages, many containing passages devoted to understanding and knowledge.[2] But even this pales in comparison to the ultimate self-revelation: the coming of Jesus, God made flesh. This act above all others offers proof that God longs to be known—not simply as the righteous moral Governor of the universe, but as Friend and Lover.

It is God's detailed communication that allows us to relate to Him in this way. Jesus' mission was not to deliver a long list of principles and then leave the scene. It was to embody the light of those principles, ministering into real-life situations—at weddings, in the marketplace, in the wilderness.

So it should be with those who serve His cause today. God is not looking for professional scholars who will spend their careers interpreting generalities. He is calling everyday people to minister specific grace.

And what about us? Do we really know Christ? Have we come to recognize the certain sound of His voice? If so, why does so much of our spiritual communication, especially in the arenas of prayer and worship, tend to digress into the third person? Remember the song "Let's Just Praise the Lord"? Instead of actually praising the Lord, we sang *about* praising the Lord. While there is nothing wrong with admonishing one another to take appropriate action, at some point we ought to get on with it. If we have an intimate relationship with Christ, we will spend a lot of time singing and praying in the first person. We are talking *to* Jesus. There is a focus and specificity to our communion.

Hiding in Abstraction

Often the reason we are not eager to hear a specific word from God is that specificity obligates us. It terminates our spiritual playtime by exposing our hiding places. It forces us to a moment of choice: Will we follow God or will we indulge our own interests?

The opposite of a specific obedience is a form of "godliness." Many people use the trappings of Christianity to garnish self-centered lifestyles. They go to church because it is culturally appropriate or because their guilt over not doing so would spoil their Sunday afternoons. Some even find God's house a convenient, if daring, hiding place, an exquisite example of the dual meaning of *sanctuary.*

Malcolm Muggeridge, the acerbic British social critic who found Christ late in life, observed that

> one of the most effective defensive systems against God's incursions has hitherto been organized religion. The various churches have provided a refuge for fugitives from God—his voice drowned in the chanting, his smell lost in the incense, his purpose obscured and confused in creeds, dogmas, dissertations and other priestly pronunciamentos. In vast cathedrals, as in little conventicles, or just wrapped in Quaker silence, one could get away from God.[3]

There are people who listen to sermons about sin every week of their lives but have never been preached to as sinners. Nobody has ever loved them enough to ask, "Brother or sister, how is your soul?" Does this bother them? Are they sorry to be surrounded by theoretical preaching and superficial fellowship? Not at all! By participating in this arrangement, they can live for themselves and yet appear to be living for God. They are under no obligation to do or to change a thing.

This is the problem with abstract theology: People cannot live it. It is useful only as a moral cover or as an object of debate. Once doctrine becomes separated from what it is intended to promote—namely, intimate relationship with Christ—it becomes a stumbling block. The labyrinthine possibilities become an intellectual aphrodisiac that stimulates an almost mathematical approach to faith.

Theories are honed and polished but, like vintage cars, rarely driven. Their owners are too obsessed with protecting them. All the while character remains unchanged, or even deteriorates.

Abstract guidance is no better than abstract doctrine, and for much the same reason. Its design, or at least its effect, is to relieve us of the heat and responsibility of specifics. It affords us maneuver room.

While this type of guidance may suit us, God will not cooperate. He refuses to allow His will to be made into a coloring book in which we fill in the details according to our own discretion. He insists we do things His way.

God's way is to address reality. He does not compromise, equivocate or dispense polite hints. His approach is penetrating and often uncomfortable. For this reason those who serve as His mouthpieces are more likely to be rejected with violence than received as deliverers. John the Baptist found this out when he was imprisoned for rebuking Herod's adultery (see Luke 3:19–20). Stephen's impassioned preaching led to his furious stoning at the hands of the Sanhedrin (see Acts 7:51–58), while Paul's ministry before the same group provoked a murder conspiracy (see Acts 23:12–15). Even Jesus was abandoned at the height of His popularity when He began to emphasize the cost of discipleship (see John 6:48–66). Such is the price true ministers must pay for refusing to allow people to hide in abstraction.[4]

Authority Must Be Manifested

God's certain sound is not only specific, it is authoritative. It can calm the fiercest storm and bestow credibility on the simplest ministry. Those who bear this trademark need not prove themselves through political maneuvering or publicity campaigns. In the words of Chicago pastor John Eckhardt, "If you are [a messenger of God], then as you preach and teach, your gift will be evident. Others in the body will perceive the grace given unto you (see Galatians 2:9)."[5]

A number of years ago I attended an evangelistic training school in Europe. Midway through the program, a visiting speaker launched a week of teaching with the following statement: "I'm going to share a number of concepts with you this week. If you like them, keep them. If you don't like them, throw them away. If you don't know what to do with them, put them on the shelf."

As this dear man continued with his lecture, I could not help imagining Jesus concluding His Sermon on the Mount in similar fashion: "Folks, if you like what you've heard, take it with you. If it offends you, just ignore it. If you're not sure what to do with it, slip it into your knapsack."

How different this is from the true Christ! How incompatible with the record of Matthew 7:28–29:

> When Jesus had finished saying these things, the crowds were amazed at his teaching, because he taught as one who had *authority*, and not as their teachers of the law.
>
> emphasis added

There was a dimension to the teachings and ministry of Jesus unlike anything that had come before. It was, in a word, *authoritative*.

The words *authoritative* and *interpretive* are not synonymous. Whereas the former is confident and assertive ("God says"), the latter is cautious and tentative ("This appears to be what God is saying"). Both concepts have their place, but we must acknowledge their differences.

Authority cannot merely be claimed; it must be manifested. The people were astonished at Jesus' doctrine because He taught them as one having *authority*. This, as we have seen, was in marked contrast to their teachers of the law, whose primary aim was to interpret God to the common man. The Pharisees had kept the people in tow for years by claiming to be official representatives of the royal household. Now Jesus bounded into the synagogue and said, "I don't represent the royal household, I'm family!" It was nothing short of revolutionary.

Besides being ego-deflating, Jesus' claims were damaging to the Pharisees' core business. He simply had to go. The problem was the miracles. At almost every turn, someone was shouting His name. Blind eyes were being opened, cripples were being put back on their feet and lepers were being transformed into walking billboards for divine skin care. But the case that really disturbed the establishment was Lazarus. What do you say when a man who has been dead for three days emerges from his burial chamber? This was authority manifested, a supernatural deed validating a supernatural message.

The Pharisees were down on all counts. Not only were they bereft of miracles, but their lack of intimacy with the Lawgiver meant that even their interpreting lacked authority. It was a zero sum game: no power, no authority and no meaningful response.

When Moses passed his mantle of leadership on to Joshua, he also presented his faithful lieutenant with the unenviable

task of following one of the greatest leaders in history. I have
often wondered how Joshua assumed authority over the unruly
Hebrews. Did he just blow a trumpet fanfare and claim his
crown? "Men and women of Israel, I have assumed the mantle of the great prophet Moses, and I am going to lead you
into the Promised Land." I can just see those burly, unshaven
Jewish men looking outside their tents and saying, "Who does
this fellow think he is?"

This scenario might well have become history had not
Moses laid hands on his young aide. As it turned out, God
used this act to fill Joshua with a "spirit of wisdom"—a wisdom manifesting such authority that "the Israelites listened
to him" (Deuteronomy 34:9). At the conclusion of his stirring
inaugural speech, the people responded:

> "Whatever you have commanded us we will do, and wherever
> you send us we will go. Just as we fully obeyed Moses, so we will
> obey you. Only may the Lord your God be with you as he was
> with Moses."
>
> Joshua 1:16–17

A similar case of manifest authority is recorded in 1 Samuel
11. It, too, concerns the rise of an anointed but unproven
leader—Saul the Benjamite. His antagonist in the story is
Nahash, a powerful Ammonite warlord who had besieged the
Jewish community at Jabesh Gilead.

Fearing for their lives, the men of Jabesh set out to nego-
tiate a treaty with Nahash. Unfortunately they had little lever-
age, since Israel at the time had no central authority and no
organized army. The Ammonite held all the cards, and Nahash
knew it. His reply in verse 2 reveals the twisted nature of his
character:

> "I will make a treaty with you only on the condition that I gouge
> out the right eye of every one of you and so bring disgrace on all
> Israel."

Faced with these sadistic terms, the elders of Jabesh issued a final, desperate counterproposal:

> "Give us seven days so we can send messengers throughout Israel; if no one comes to rescue us, we will surrender to you."
>
> verse 3

That Nahash even considered this audacious appeal reveals his utter contempt for the Israelites' prospects. His experience told him that no one could rally those sorry tribes, even if they were granted seven *months* to do it.

One thing the warlord did not account for was the certain sound of God's authority. It proved a fatal oversight. The Bible recounts that when Saul heard news of Nahash's cruel proposition, "the Spirit of God came upon him in power, and he burned with anger" (verse 6). Ripping apart a pair of oxen, he ordered couriers to pick up the pieces and carry them throughout Israel. Each grisly package was to be accompanied by the same message:

> "This is what will be done to the oxen of anyone who does not follow Saul and Samuel."
>
> verse 7

It may have been the most effective mailgram in history. Throughout the land, we are told, "the terror of the LORD fell on the people, and they turned out as one man" (verse 7). Three hundred and thirty thousand warriors mustered at Bezek against the Ammonites, every one of them conscripted by the manifest authority of God.

The power of divine authenticity is further seen in the public reactions to Solomon's adjudication of the case involving the infant with two mothers (see 1 Kings 3:28); Jesus' preaching on the road to Emmaus (see Luke 24:32); and Peter's stirring Pentecost sermon (see Acts 2:37).

Sadly modern-day preaching is rarely this penetrating. This is because, in the quest for our attention, form has supplanted substance. Contemporary ministers are so polished they even seem to sweat right. Many have developed a stage actor's walk, along with the ability to modulate their voices for maximum effect. Others can turn a phrase worthy of the best Roman orators. But the questions remain: Is this divine authority or well-rehearsed showmanship? Is it the anointing of God or the projection of personality? Can we even tell the difference?

Learning God's Voice

In the mid-1970s I attended a spiritual leadership conference at a mountain retreat near Santa Cruz, California. One of the featured speakers was Campbell McAlpine, an anointed Bible teacher from Worthing, England. His vivid messages illumined the ways and purposes of God and always left me wanting more. On one particular morning something unusual happened. As Campbell concluded one of his trademark messages, he shifted seamlessly into a powerful prophetic exhortation. Within thirty seconds the entire audience was prostrate before God. So palpable was the Spirit's presence that no one dared stay seated. The word was direct, sobering and intimate. It cut to the core of our hearts. Even Campbell lay prostrate on the platform sobbing before God. No one was left to wonder whether the message was authentic.

Over the course of my life I have heard many "prophetic" words delivered in God's name. To be frank, very few have struck me as genuine. Most came across as nice, well-intentioned messages that lacked the authority of the Holy Spirit. Instead of sending congregations falling to their faces in awe, they elicited thankful murmurs and ill-timed yawns.

Why do we suffer these dubious deliveries? One major reason is that many pastors lack the courage to bring necessary teaching and discipline to their congregations. Some are afraid of stifling the Holy Spirit, while others worry about offending their parishioners. The result is a growing confusion between flesh and spirit.

People are rarely drawn to charismatic ministries because they have discerned the mark of God's authority or because they are eager to hear a penetrating word. More often than not, the attraction is something far more basic: a lively style or atmosphere. The problem with this trend is that charisma and enthusiasm cannot substitute for authority. Nor, for that matter, can knowledge, opinion or persuasiveness. Adolf Hitler and Mao Zedong possessed all these qualities, and used them to turn millions of ordinary citizens into ruthless killers.

Christians who fail to look for God's trademarks run the risk of being led down a primrose path, separated from their pocketbooks and their common sense. Their teachers will speak great, billowing words but never lead them to the truth. Indeed, if we are to believe the great Christian pastor and writer A. W. Tozer, this dark scenario has already enveloped the Church of Jesus Christ:

> The church is in her Babylonian captivity, and as Israel could not sing the songs of Zion in a strange land, so Christians in bondage have no authoritative message to declare.[6]

Many of us struggle to discern spiritual authenticity because we have not spent intimate time with the Lord. We have religious experience but no real relationship with the One who is our original standard of comparison. We have not yet noticed that authority has the word *author* embedded in its core.

To remedy this situation—an absolute must if we harbor any hopes of recognizing or delivering authoritative ministry—we must get to know the Author of truth. In John 10:2–5 Jesus told His followers:

"The man who enters by the gate is the shepherd of his sheep. The watchman opens the gate for him, and the sheep listen to his voice. He calls his own sheep by name and leads them out. When he has brought out all his own, he goes on ahead of them, and his sheep follow him because *they know his voice*. But they will never follow a stranger; in fact, they will run away from him because *they do not recognize a stranger's voice*."

emphasis added

Do we have this kind of relationship with Christ? When we speak to Him, does He lean forward? When He speaks to us, do we lean forward?[7] Have we come to know the certain sound of His character and personality? Do we know it well enough to avoid the voice of strangers?

THREE

THE OPEN BOOK

The only way you can truly control how you're seen is by being honest all the time.

Tom Hanks[1]

Discussions about honesty occur millions of times a day and in a thousand different places. Mothers talk to daughters about new boyfriends; storeowners talk to clerks about shady customers; middle-aged men talk to their barbers about politicians. Most of these conversations, especially those involving public figures or budding relationships, are punctuated by personal anecdotes and time-tested aphorisms.

Two of the more common adages are *You can't always judge a book by its cover* and *What you see is what you get*. The first aims to remind listeners of the wisdom of suspended judgment, while the latter asserts that appearance is reality—that first impressions reflect ultimate truth. Whereas the former is generalized and objective, the second depends almost entirely on the veracity of the declarer.

The benefits of authentic intelligence are so pronounced that we often go to great lengths to obtain it. Reporters sift through the earlier speeches and voting records of political candidates; employers interview multiple references before hiring prospective employees; young women grill the acquaintances (preferably past girlfriends) of prospective love interests. Unfortunately, even when we succeed in acquiring this intelligence, it rarely provides us with the measure of certainty we seek. Most of us have learned the hard way that what we see is almost never what we get. It is safer to take the more patient approach and suspend judgment.

One of the less attractive human tendencies is that of hiding agendas. So adept are we at this game that we might well be labeled moral magicians. But here is the rub: What we are capable of doing to others, they can also do to us. Indeed this has become our ever-present worry. In budding romances, in business negotiations, in media interviews, in ministry partnerships, our thought is always the same: *How might this person hurt me?* Our posture is almost continuously defensive.

"There are few pleasanter things in life," Malcolm Muggeridge wrote in his *Chronicles of Wasted Time*, "than the companionship of a totally honest mind."[2] The question is, Where do we find such minds? If they are not altogether alien to human society, they are hardly in oversupply.

Our search for the totally honest mind must begin, as it does with all absolute virtues, with God Himself. It is only as we come unreservedly into His presence that we are able to suspend all personal intelligence-gathering and safety patrols. Relieved of this considerable burden, we can redirect our time and energy into exploration of the divine character.

God's second trademark is what I call "the open book," a manifestation of absolute honesty and integrity. Any investigation into His ways assures us that what we see is indeed what we get. But so is what we do *not* see. The depth of His character stands beyond measure—not as a dark abyss but as a glorious, incxhaustible fount. Although new revelations emerge daily, none is inconsistent with what we have come to know of God's essential Person. They are extrapolations rather than inventions. They give us reason to seek the divine unknown rather than fear it.

God is honest, but this does not make Him, as one seventeenth-century writer insinuated, a "soft easy seat cushion on which knaves repose and fatten."[3] (See Ecclesiastes 8:11 and Zephaniah 1:12 about the perils of deferred judgment.) Rather, as C. S. Lewis wrote in *The Lion, the Witch and the Wardrobe*, "[He] is a lion—*the* Lion, the great Lion."

> "Ooh!" said Susan, "I'd thought he was a man. Is he—quite safe? I shall feel rather nervous about meeting a lion."
>
> "That you will, dearie, and no mistake," said Mrs. Beaver, "if there's anyone who can appear before Aslan without their knees knocking, they're either braver than most or else just silly."
>
> "Then he isn't safe?" said Lucy.
>
> "Safe?" said Mr. Beaver. "Don't you hear what Mrs. Beaver tells you? Who said anything about safe? 'Course he isn't safe. But he's good. He's the King, I tell you."
>
> "I'm longing to see him," said Peter, "even if I do feel frightened. . . ."[4]

In another of his books, Lewis calls this reaction "numinous awe."[5] It is the undefined sense of God's true presence, something at once terrifying and indescribably glorious:

> . . . It was the Jews who fully and unambiguously identified the awful Presence haunting the black mountain-tops and thunderclouds with "the righteous Lord" who "loveth righteousness" . . . (Ps. 11:7). There was a man born among these Jews who claimed to be, or to be the son of, or to be "one with," the Something which is at once the awful haunter of nature and the giver of the moral law.[6]

Looking under the Cover

It has been rightly said that a good book contains more wealth than a good bank. Its abundant riches can include life-tested knowledge, fresh inspiration and the wondrous ability to transport us to realms both real and imaginary. Before we can mine this wealth, however, we must first determine whether a particular volume is good.

Covers, as the old adage reminds us, are of little help. Their appealing art and splendid endorsements may encourage us to review a particular book, or even buy it, but they cannot settle the question of its intrinsic value. Covers are designed to attract our attention, not provide us with an objective analysis of the chapters inside.

Not surprisingly, handsome dust jackets can occasionally mislead us as to a book's true subject matter. They can also camouflage limited or substandard content. The only way to avoid this deception (and any resulting disappointment) is to crack the cover and read the fine print.

While this is easily accomplished with bound volumes, people are an altogether different matter. Human beings have more at stake and are often reluctant to grant outsiders access to their true selves. Many have weaknesses or sins they wish to conceal. Others simply want to maintain a false (and often inflated) public perception of their true character, abilities, accomplishments or intentions.

So pervasive is this tendency toward self-concealment and "character spin" that one might wonder if *any* ministry is truly knowable. Some, like eighteenth-century playwright Susanna Centlivre, are pessimistic. "He is only honest who is not discovered," she wrote in *The Artifice*.[7] While this judgment skirts the far edge of cynicism, it is an understandable response to what has become a disturbing pattern of behavior among Christian leaders and their organizations.

Many ministers are open and engaging until they are asked the wrong question. This can be something as simple as "What are your sources on that story?" or "How are you balancing ministry and family life?" or "Do you have an independently audited financial statement?" No sooner are these words out of our mouths than their demeanor darkens like an approaching thunderstorm. They want us to look *at* their cover, not lift it.

Those who claim accountability but secretly despise it generally have something to hide (or at least wish to reserve the right to do so). I can think of three people—among them a prominent televangelist, a popular Christian musician and a well-known radio apologist—who have lately worked hard to dismiss inquiries into their lavish lifestyles. I know of a still-presiding pastor of a large Northwest church who was inadvertently photographed exiting a XXX adult theater. While it is not for me to condemn these individuals, their stories provide yet another reminder that the contents of a book does not always match its cover. They are like the woman who tattooed her makeup on so she would never look less than perfect. As long as the public keeps its distance and she does not weep, no one is the wiser.

Repentant pornography entrepreneur Steve Lane once trolled for customers in Christian online chat rooms. "I kept a record of how many of them subscribed to the site," he now says regretfully. "[It was] probably five out of ten." Lane believes pornography is a dirty little secret that plagues many Christian leaders, particularly men. "I have known churches where everything looked good: the worship, the tithes, the new seat covers and the banners—but no one in the church had a clue that their own pastor was defeated for 20 years by pornography. . . ." Lane's own descent into lust and anger began in his childhood when his mother was drawn into an affair with his pastor, whom she later married. What no one else knew about this fire-and-brimstone preacher was that he was deeply addicted to smut. "It looked like the perfect Christian home from the outside," Lane recalls, "but from the inside my life was hell."[8]

The godly servant cannot be two-faced. As Jesus told His disciples, "The student [must] be like his teacher, and the servant like his master" (Matthew 10:25). Our lives should allow us to declare with Christ, "Anyone who has seen me has seen the Father" (John 14:9). Those who examine our stories should find no other cover and no other chapter. When nothing of self is concealed, there is no need to fear awkward disclosures (see Luke 12:2). Characterized by moral transparency, we can say, "The ruler of this world is coming, [but] he has nothing in Me" (John 14:30, NKJV).

Godly messengers and institutions will never be put off by investigations into their character. Indeed openness is one of their prime trademarks. They invite the world in for a closer look because they want it to see, and then embrace, genuine honesty and integrity. This is why the apostle Paul could say, "Imitate me, just as I also imitate Christ" (1 Corinthians 11:1, NKJV; see also Philippians 3:17; 4:9). As he explained in his first epistle to the Corinthians:

> When I came to you, brothers, I did not come with eloquence or superior wisdom as I proclaimed to you the testimony about God. . . . My message and my preaching were not with wise and persuasive words, but with a demonstration of the Spirit's power, so that your faith might not rest on men's wisdom, but on God's power.
>
> 1 Corinthians 2:1, 4–5

This same open and humble approach is now advocated by Ann Kiemel Anderson, one of America's most popular Christian communicators. In her refreshingly honest book *Seduced by Success*, Anderson admits her new outlook is the product of a near shipwrecked marriage and a secret addiction to pain pills. "I had to learn that best-selling books and standing ovations don't make a person whole," she says. "God had to deliver me from myself."[9]

Let Your Yea Be Yea

Christians who wish to retain their focus and resources are often forced to bushwhack their way through a dense thicket of half-truths and hidden agendas. Almost nothing in this modern jungle is what it seems. Those who tend its shadows manifest delusions of grandeur and the pretense of caring. They spin illusions of depth and celebrate ephemeral success. Missing altogether is genuine wisdom, sincerity, commitment and accomplishment.

As William Bennett has noted in *The Book of Virtues*, "Dishonesty seeks shade, cover, or concealment. It is a disposition to live partly in the dark."[10] Dishonest people are jungle people. They need the shadows and dappled light to create illusions. They "believe lies," Muggeridge wrote in *The Green Stick*, "not because they are plausibly presented, but because they want to believe them."[11]

Open book people, on the other hand, eschew deception in any form. They refuse to manipulate, exaggerate or entertain hidden agendas. Their positions do not vacillate, nor are their commitments written in disappearing ink. They take seriously Jesus' admonition to "simply let your 'Yes' be 'Yes,' and your 'No,' 'No,'" realizing that "anything beyond this comes from the evil one" (Matthew 5:37).

Sadly, writes Tozer, "Many of our best-known preachers and teachers have developed ventriloquial tongues and can now make their voices come from any direction."[12] John White adds that the same might be said of various ministry executives whose appeals for financial assistance are often coded and circuitous. To ascertain their real meanings, we are often forced to read between the lines.

The words *by faith* [have] acquired a technical meaning and [now] constitute a badge of spiritual respectability. Today we scarcely smile at the inconsistency of a Christian radio program closing with the words, "As you know this is a venture of faith. We are looking to God alone to meet all our needs, as you his people give generously to support this effort which reaches millions of needy people with the gospel. Our program costs $50,000 weekly. Please write and encourage us. Your letters mean so much. . . . We would like to send you at no charge a booklet entitled. . . ." And so on.[13]

Mature Christians understand that since God has a stake in the success of each message and mission He ordains, He can be relied on to prepare the way for His servants. He is a master at softening the hearts of the lost and stirring the hearts of donors. There is no need for ministers to beat around the bush—and those who do reveal either a lack of confidence in God's calling or the presence of a hidden agenda.

Slippery Facts

Equivocators often migrate into the company of exaggerators. Their unwillingness to stick to the truth makes them easy companions for those who stretch it. An initial tolerance of slippery facts gives way to selective deception, and eventually to full-fledged "reality modification."

Christian leaders and fundraisers endeavoring to sustain enormous campaigns are sorely tempted in this area. Having promised their supporters the moon, they must either deliver big or lose their seat on the gravy train. The problem, of course, is that the needs of the real world are too large and too complex to be addressed by any one organization. The only solution (other than honesty) is to downsize the challenge by means of ambiguous program titles (Africa for Christ, The Billion Souls Campaign) and dubious statistics (usually related to *estimated* crusade attendance or *potential* broadcast coverage). Both devices can be pushed to the limit because of the inherent difficulty in verifying their actual intent or effectiveness.

This airbrushing of reality is all the more impressive when it includes foreign scenes. "Indeed," Muggeridge wrote in his autobiography, "one marvels at the almost mystical importance attached to the location of a news-gatherer as distinct from the truthfulness of the news sent."[14] Add to this instinctive credulity the considerable time and expense required to check out distant facts, and it is easy to see why dishonest operators are so fond of international programs.

John White recounts an example of a Christian organization that coached its workers to set evangelistic quotas and then package the new converts' testimonies as "war stories" for publication. Yet, according to one worker, "The ink would scarcely be dry on the paper before most of the converts had ditched their 'faith.'" This was said to happen constantly. As White points out, the information in the prayer letter was misleading. "The stories that appeared in the letter were not the stories being told when the letter was read."[15]

This account, and others like it, should prompt us to ask some important questions. First and most obvious, Was the advancement of this organization a higher priority than the extension of God's Kingdom? Did it lead ministry executives to compromise scriptural standards of truth? Is this the "greed" the apostle Peter warned would cause some Christian leaders to "exploit [us] with stories they have made up" (2 Peter 2:3)?

Wooing versus Manipulation

Many believers find it difficult to distinguish between the wooing of the Holy Spirit and human manipulation. Both approaches stimulate the mind and emotions, and both call us to support apparently worthy causes. There is, however, a profound difference: Spiritual wooing is gentle, respectful and honest, while manipulation views people as objects to be exploited. One is relationally oriented while the other is program-oriented.

It must be acknowledged that, in many instances, manipulation works. In fact, an entire industry has grown up around its practice and propagation. Pollsters discover what people are thinking and feeling; publishers deliver the results to our desktops and nightstands; and consultants and seminar hosts teach us how to exploit what we know.

With so many Christians embracing this calculated approach to ministry, it may be time for us to ask whether we are children of God or children of science. White worries that many of our modern methods may actually undermine faith in the Holy Spirit. While advertising and persuasion are not intrinsically evil, they can nevertheless cause great harm "when the motive for using them is greed or when in using them we fail to treat human beings as human, ignore their dignity, and view them as objects to manipulate."[16]

Are we able to declare with Paul that "we have renounced secret and shameful ways"? Can we attest that "we do not use deception, nor do we distort the word of God"? Are we prepared to employ unvarnished truth to "commend ourselves to every man's conscience in the sight of God" (2 Corinthians 4:2)?

Although psychological manipulation can sometimes yield short-lived results, it is no match for the wooing and conviction of the Holy Spirit. The people of Jerusalem did not need an altar call at the end of Peter's Pentecost sermon. There were no breathless whispers to "seize this special moment." No organist played the soft strains of "I Surrender All." Instead, the Bible tells us the crowds "were cut to the heart" and immediately confronted Peter and the other apostles with the question, "Brothers, what shall we do?" (Acts 2:37). When it was all over, three thousand souls had been added to the Church. "Everyone," we are told, "was filled with awe" (verse 43). This is not to impugn the validity of altar calls per se. Rather it is a reminder that we should let the Bridegroom do the wooing.

The manner in which a person is sought is indicative of his or her suitor's intentions. If the objective is a one-night stand (a tallied hand, an impulsive donation), then manipulation will prevail. But if our ultimate aim is marriage (a firm disciple, a long-term partner), then we will need to woo our lover's heart.

Many of us are not honest before men because we are not honest before God. We carry private ambitions and secret sins—"the hidden things of darkness" that must one day be revealed (1 Corinthians 4:5, NKJV). But God desires truth in our "inner parts" (Psalm 51:6), and He makes clear that any attempt to conceal our sin will not prosper (see Proverbs 28:13).

If our lives are to be an open book, our only hope is to cry with David, "Search me, O God, and know my heart" (Psalm 139:23), and with Job, "Teach me what I cannot see" (Job 34:32).[17] It is only as we ourselves are tried and refined that we are able to recognize pretense in others.

FOUR

THE REFLECTED THRONE

Our whole destiny seems to lie in . . . acquiring a fragrance that is not our own but borrowed, in becoming clean mirrors filled with the image of a face that is not ours.

C. S. Lewis[1]

The Bible not only allows that there is "a time to laugh" (Ecclesiastes 3:4); it even tells us why. "A merry heart," it turns out, "does good, like medicine" (Proverbs 17:22, NKJV). One who understands this better than anyone is my dear friend and colleague Alistair Petrie. On more than one occasion I have watched this Spirit-filled Anglican vicar send audiences into convulsions with a dry wit and comedic timing.

One humorous anecdote he tells involves a certain family that became fed up with the noise and traffic of the city and decided to move to the country, to try life in the wide-open spaces. Intending to raise cattle, they bought a Western ranch. Some friends came to visit a month later and asked them what they had named their new spread.

"Well, it got a little complicated," the father said, rubbing his chin. "I wanted to call it the Flying-W but my wife wanted to name it the Suzy-Q."

"So which one did you settle on?" the friends asked interestedly.

"As a matter of fact, these weren't the *only* alternatives," the father replied. "Our older son liked the Bar-J, and the younger one preferred the Lazy-Y."

"So what in the world did you do?" the visitors probed.

"Well, we compromised and called it the Flying-W, Suzy-Q, Bar-J, Lazy-Y Ranch."

Stifling their laughter, the friends asked, "Well, where are your cattle?"

Looking down, the man replied, "None of them survived the branding!"[2]

Not so funny is the fact that a type of "lethal branding" is now a widespread practice in Christian circles. Many ministry leaders are no longer interested in God's trademarks but are instead scrambling to affix their own names to high-profile programs and events. Not infrequently the brands seared onto these initiatives are so numerous that the program's initial intent and momentum are overwhelmed, and it eventually dies.

Sadly, few leaders really care about these deaths. By the time the program or movement finally collapses, it has already served its purpose—either as a convenient cash cow or as public advertising for their well-connected ministries. Their interests are limited to a comfortable journey with sufficient admirers. They are people of means—but not ends.

The Spirit of "Peacock-ism"

The Christian Church, particularly in the West, has entered a season in which narcissism and self-adulation have become dominant features of the religious landscape. Never before has such competitive pressure been seen and heard. At almost every turn Christian authors, pastors, musicians and evangelists have succumbed to a condition my good friend Ken Eldred calls the "spirit of peacock-ism."

To grasp the meaning of this term we need look no further than the modern conference platform or television studio set. It is here we find the "anointed ones," the peak performers, the acclaimed celebrities of the hour. Turn on the klieg lights and they will preen for the camera; turn on the sound system and they will stir the emotions of adoring audiences. Although they are introduced as humble Kingdom servants, their "look at me" demeanor and overeager grasp of the microphone leads one to wonder just who is being served.

Concerns about judging frequently prevent us from acknowledging the behaviors that set these operators apart from the many dedicated and selfless Christian communicators of our day. Aware of our own flaws, we are willing to rationalize the private jets and half-million-dollar touring coaches that bring these spiritual celebrities to us. We may not appreciate the need for entourages that rival small armies but neither will we criticize them. Ditto the fabulously expensive sets and garish wardrobes. As Pascal says, judges need their wigs and robes, priests their vestments, scholars their gowns.[3] So Christian artists need their long hair and facial stubble, televangelists and crusade personalities their Armani suits and well-folded handkerchiefs.

Gazing out decades ago on the rising tide of vainglory, A. W. Tozer remarked that it is as if "Christ now stands in need of a patron, a celebrity who will sponsor Him before the world." If He cannot find such a "well-known figure upon whose inside popularity He can ride forth," His cause will be greatly diminished, if not lost altogether.[4]

But who is truly concerned about His cause? Has anything changed since Paul lamented, "Everyone looks out for his own interests, not those of Jesus Christ" (Philippians 2:21)?

The ranks of Christian speakers and musicians have increasingly been filled with demanding prima donnas whose bookings are based on prestigious venues and ample honoraria. Many no longer even bother to pray over their invitations. Their first and only thought is, *How do I come out?*

These same high-service egos are also found among pastors and ministry leaders, many of whom are so busy designing new programs and sanctuaries they have practically no contact with their constituencies. Like spiritual sahibs they spend their existence in the privileged isolation of studies, executive suites and "green rooms," venturing out only rarely—and always with fitting pomp and protocol—for worship services, staff meetings and fundraising banquets.

Nor are Christian publishers free of this infectious self-interest. While many claim to be dedicated purveyors of spiritually enriching content, their editorial decision-making suggests economic opportunism. (Can anyone say with a straight face that God ordained the recent spate of Y2K books? Or that these titles were published for *His* benefit?) Once again spiritual standards have been suspended in favor of earthly gain.

Hail to the sales charts! Hail to the attendance rolls! Hail to the bank account! Hail to the press release! We have become people of measure, and our standard is success. Hear the ambitious pastor dedicate his newly minted sanctuary; listen to the television mogul introduce his latest network affiliate. An ancient sound has entered the land, and it is none other than Nebuchadnezzar's rooftop boast: "Is not this the great Babylon I have built as the royal residence, by my mighty power and for the glory of my majesty?" (Daniel 4:30).

We have become people of success—but by whose standard are we measured? Are we satisfied with human adulation born of accomplishment, or do we seek the quiet favor of God? It is not a question of our natural tendency, which is to pursue greatness in the eyes of men; it is a question of what is right and real and biblical. If we are serious about attracting God's favor, we

can start with the admonition of Philippians 2:3–4: "Do nothing out of selfish ambition or vain conceit, but in humility consider others better than yourselves. Each of you should look not
only to your own interests, but also to the interests of others."[5]

Bad Directions and Lost Signals

The defenders of today's colorful ministries encourage us
to examine results rather than flaws. They insist we not throw
the proverbial baby out with the bath water. Celebrity rap concerts may not be our cup of tea, but if they are what it takes
to draw people into church . . . If we are disturbed that Christian conferences are headlining notable prophets and faith-
healers, well, maybe we should lighten up. There is nothing
wrong with a little marquee value. The Church has her stars,
and God knows how to use them.

This argument has troubled many observers in recent years,
perhaps none more so than the godly preacher A. W. Tozer.
Writing in *The Set of the Sail,* he declared:

> The Church in America suffered a greater loss than she [has yet
> realized] when she rejected the example of good men and chose
> for her pattern the celebrity of the hour.[6]

Tozer rued the fact that Christians, like their worldly counterparts, are now measuring human greatness by means of
popularity polls, press coverage and material accomplishments.
For this very reason, he said,

> It is altogether unlikely that we know who our greatest men are
> . . . for the holy man is also the humble man and the humble man
> will not advertise himself nor allow others to do it for him.[7]

Despite Peter's injunction to spiritual leaders that they not
pursue ministry for glory or "sordid gain" (1 Peter 5:2, NASB),

the Church today is awash in human vanity and self-promo-
tion. Our preachers, singers and television personalities strut
like princelings or peacocks—not because they are servants of
the Most High God but because they are able to draw the
masses. And while some would have us believe this is but a
trifling matter, in fact it calls into question a man or woman's
very suitability for ministry.

Consider Paul's declaration to the Corinthians:

> When I came to you, brothers, I did not come with eloquence
> or superior wisdom as I proclaimed to you the testimony about
> God. For I resolved to know nothing while I was with you except
> Jesus Christ and him crucified. *I came to you in weakness* and fear,
> and with much trembling. My message *and my preaching* were
> not with wise and persuasive words, but with a demonstration of
> the Spirit's power, *so that your faith might not rest on men's wis-
> dom*, but on God's power.
>
> 1 Corinthians 2:1–5, emphasis added

The suggestion here is that our ministry approach has a
direct influence on the foundation of our listeners' faith. If we
want to produce disciples rather than mere converts, we will
have to give thoughtful consideration not only to our message
but also to our style of preaching (see verse 4). And the best
style is one that reflects an attitude of humility:

> Brothers, think of what you were when you were called. Not many
> of you were wise by human standards; not many were influential;
> not many were of noble birth. But God chose the foolish things
> of the world to shame the wise; God chose the weak things of the
> world to shame the strong. He chose the lowly things of this world
> and the despised things—and the things that are not—to nullify
> the things that are, so that no one may boast before him.
>
> 1 Corinthians 1:26–29

Tozer contended that "the preacher who loves to be before
the public is hardly prepared spiritually to be before them."

Indeed, he wrote, "No man should stand before an audience who has not first stood [or knelt] before God."[8] It is in the solemn presence of the Almighty that boisterous peacocks are transformed into gentle doves (see Proverbs 11:2).

The greater an individual's talent or ambition, the more he or she must learn to say with Jeremiah, "I know, O LORD, that a man's life is not his own; it is not for man to direct his steps" (Jeremiah 10:23). Absent this crucial revelation, we will only misdirect pilgrims on the road to truth.

A godly message or ministry will point heavenward as surely as a compass needle spins toward the true north. It will focus attention on the Way, never on elegant vehicles, colorful scenery or useless diversions. It will encourage us to stay our course by reflecting, however briefly and imperfectly, the glories of our destination.

The reflected throne is one of heaven's most distinctive trademarks. It is also one of the surest ways to ascertain the spiritual authenticity of a given ministry or messenger. Those who exhibit this characteristic invariably eschew any accolade or action that might obscure God's glory. They understand that when human attention is focused on human agency, it is necessarily drawn away from reality. And from that very moment the messenger ceases to minister and starts to entertain.

Given this understanding, it is sobering to note the high number of ministries that remain messenger-centric. Indeed many bear as their title the very name of their founder or principal performer. Others post flattering (and unending) photos of their resident heroes on everything from websites and newsletters to catalogs and product covers. Valued partners or parishioners are invited to share in the glory of preaching to multitudes on the foreign field, dedicating new churches or television stations and shaking hands with various Christian and secular dignitaries.

This messenger-centric approach is the one characteristic Christian ministries have in common with most cults. Messages are linked so inextricably with personalities that it is impossible to get the one without a heavy dose of the other. To contend that this intertwining is "only a matter of style" is to miss the point entirely. The reassurances of preachers, pastors, prophets and presidents cannot erase one fundamental fact: Whenever the medium takes precedence over the message, the "servant" is drawing attention to himself.

Sitting under these ministries is like asking the wrong person for directions. We want to get to the truth, but are instead steered toward unreality. Some of us will waste precious time reorienting ourselves; others will never reach their intended destination at all.

For true servants of God this scenario is a full-blown nightmare. The very idea of causing someone to lose contact with his or her Maker sends chills up their spines. It is analogous to switching off a fog-bound pilot's radar or cutting the life-support cables of a deep-sea diver. They would rather give their own lives than be responsible for the loss of such intimate and life-sustaining signals. Their cry is that of David who said:

> Not to us, O LORD, not to us
> but to your name be the glory,
> because of your love and faithfulness.
>
> Psalm 115:1

Any truly God-honoring messenger will seek to *deflect* attention rather than *absorb* it. The prophets pointed to One who was yet to come (see Luke 3:16); the angels and apostles refused to be worshiped (see Judges 13:16; Acts 14:11–15); the Holy Spirit brought glory to Jesus (see John 16:13–14); Jesus said, "These words you hear are not my own; they belong to the Father who sent me" (John 14:24).

When John the Baptist cried out, "He must increase, but I must decrease" (John 3:30, KJV), it was not in doleful resignation over dwindling crowds. To the contrary, he spoke these words at the zenith of his ministry. Being a true servant, John was aware, and delighted, that a greater ministry had arrived on the scene. He insisted that public attention should migrate to the Christ, whose way he had come to prepare.

When a minister ceases to care about "coming off," he jettisons as unnecessary the manipulative techniques that once serviced his personal agenda. Relieved of this cumbersome load, he begins to preach, sing and write himself out of people's consciousness. His only ambition is to lead people to the Master.

My first experience with this type of "invisible ministry" took place in the mid-1970s while lecturing at a discipleship training school in Southern California. As I expounded on the nature and implications of Christ's atonement, the presence of the Holy Spirit settled on us in an extraordinary way. One by one the students began to weep—quietly at first; then, as the revelation intensified, with loud sobs. Many slipped reverently to their knees. Others gazed up to the heavens. Still others covered their faces with trembling hands. As I surveyed the audience at that moment, it was apparent that I no longer commanded anyone's attention. There was nothing left to do but gather up my notes and join the grateful chorus. It was the most premature and yet the most consummate closing I had ever experienced.

See-through Servants

Many of us talk about promoting the Kingdom, but what we really hope is that the Holy Spirit will promote us. Fortunately for God's Kingdom and His people, the Spirit has an exclusive contract to promote Christ; and Christ, not surprisingly, passes the attention onto the Father. When Jesus said to Philip, "Anyone who has seen me has seen the Father"

(John 14:9), He was drawing attention not to His sufficiency but to His transparency. He was see-through to heaven, a reflected throne, the very heart of God on exhibition.

Humility was the guiding star, the sin-subverting ethos, of Jesus' ministry. As He told the Jewish religious establishment, "I do not accept praise from men . . . [for] by myself I can do nothing; I judge only as I hear, and my judgment is just, for *I seek not to please myself but him who sent me*" (John 5:41, 30; emphasis added). As revolutionary as this modesty was in the life of Christ, it did not appear as an autumn bloom. It was present from the very beginning, at once the unifying flux and dominant theme of the sublime Christmas story.

The Nativity has lessons—and questions—for us yet. The stable where Christ would present Himself to the world is still in need of a doorkeeper. Can He count on us? Are we prepared to give ourselves to such a lowly but necessary task? Do we still wish to serve Him if it means our role will go largely unnoticed by men? Can we be as attentive to threadbare shepherds as we are to well-heeled magi? Are we willing to open the door in such a way that our shadow is not cast across the Master?

Where we stand in relation to Christ is no small question. It can determine (at least temporarily) whether and in what measure a spiritual pilgrim is able to look on the object of his or her search. If we choose to stand behind the door (like courtiers or butlers), then all will be well; but if we position ourselves in the doorway (like royalty or celebrities), His visage will be hidden. In the end Christ's profound humility has left Him vulnerable to our movements and priorities. He has left amateurs to stage-manage the appearance of a King.

If we are wise, we will not seek the limelight. We will come to realize, in the words of Pittsburgh pastor Joseph Garlington, that "the thing of which we are part is greater than the part we play." We will rejoice not in the fact that there has been an introduction, but in the One who has been introduced. If attention has been focused on Jesus, it will not matter to us who has opened the door.

While many of us strive for greatness, the burden is unnecessary. We are called to be good, not great. Of such people Tozer wrote:

> These are the first to come forward when there is work to be done and the last to go home when there is prayer to be made. They are not known beyond the borders of their own parish because there is nothing dramatic in faithfulness. . . . When they die they leave behind them a fragrance of Christ that lingers long after the cheap celebrities of the day are forgotten.[9]

Dealing with "the Anointing"

Anointing is one of the more important sub-themes of spiritual calling and service. Regrettably the attitudes and lifestyles of those who claim this divine benediction sometimes cast a shadow over its proper definition. For many Christians the term is no longer a synonym for humble service but a code word for arrogance and independence.[10] Oil, of course, is the symbol of the Holy Spirit, and the truly anointed man or woman always manifests His characteristics—most notably delivering power and uncompromising servanthood.

Notwithstanding this unfortunate conflict, the Scriptures leave no doubt that humility and anointing are co-joined. This is seen most readily in the bowed head that receives the prophet's oil, but it is also glimpsed in the oil itself—a precious substance extracted under great pressure and then poured out.

Newly anointed leaders are often in a rush to stake their claim to greatness, but this is not the pattern of Israel's first two kings. Consider Saul. A week after his anointing at the hands of Samuel, a funny thing happened on the way to the coronation. When the would-be king was called up on stage, "he was not to be found" (1 Samuel 10:21). Try as they might, the inaugural committee just could not locate the anointed one. Finally "they inquired . . . of the LORD, 'Has the man come here yet?' And the LORD said, 'Yes, he has hidden himself among the baggage'" (verse 22).

David was another reluctant sovereign. Although he, too, had been anointed by Samuel, he steadfastly refused to hasten his accession through either insider connections (see 1 Samuel 18:16–23; 20:8) or treachery (see 1 Samuel 24:1–7; 26:7–12).

Ironically David's admirable behavior toward his spiritually crippled predecessor has given rise to one of the more misunderstood (and abused) teachings on "the anointing." Many leaders have seized on David's oft-repeated refrain about not touching the Lord's anointed (see 1 Samuel 26:11) as a means of stifling disagreement and warding off genuine accountability. Their implicit message seems to be "Once anointed, always right." But if Saul's tragic story tells us anything, it is that past anointing does not guarantee the present favor of God. David may not have been willing to be his master's executioner, but he also realized that "the Spirit of the LORD had departed from Saul" (see 1 Samuel 16:14; 26:10). As Tozer once remarked:

> We should and must learn that we cannot handle holy things carelessly without suffering serious consequences. . . . By the law of just compensation the heart of the religious trifler will be destroyed by the exceeding brightness of the truth he touches.[11]

Ongoing blessing can sometimes make it appear as though a rejected ministry has retained the favor of God. Such an illusion may well have been spun when David heard Saul prophesy in Samuel's presence at Naioth. But as the late Bible teacher John Wright Follette observed, "[God] often blesses in *spite* of and not *because* of the instrument or methods. . . ." He does this "because of His Word, and [because of] the hungry hearts in faith seeking Him."[12]

If spiritual anointing is not to be sought for its own sake, the favor of God most decidedly *is*. To obtain it, however, we must remember the Holy One is moved by neither endless petitions nor daring exploits. The only sure route to His heart is through obedience and humility. If we insist on the adulation that comes from power, fame and giftedness, we will never know His pleasure. As Jesus asked the Jews, "How can you believe if you accept praise from one another, yet make no effort to obtain the praise that comes from the only God?" (John 5:44).

God's timeless pattern is to take the lowly and exalt the humble. Moses was raised out of a reed basket and inarticulate speech to become one of the greatest leaders of all time. When he asked, "Who am I?" (Exodus 3:11), Yahweh responded, "I AM WHO I AM" (verse 14). In similar fashion Gideon inquired of God, "How can I save Israel? My clan is the weakest in Manasseh, and I am the least in my family" (Judges 6:15). David was a shepherd who called himself "a flea" (1 Samuel 24:14; 26:20); Peter was a backwater fisherman.

Although Paul's citizenship and education made him a notable exception to this pattern, even he viewed himself as "the least of the apostles" (1 Corinthians 15:9). When he instructed others to "follow" or "imitate" him (see 1 Corinthians 11:1; Philippians 3:17), he meant only that they should pursue the Christ who governed his affairs. Paul, too, was a "see-through servant."

And where is this attitude today? As we evaluate the authenticity of a myriad messages and ministries, our first question must always be, Where is the focus of attention? Where does the messenger want the focus of attention to be? Where do *we* want it to be?

A true ministry will lead heavenward. It is the destination, not the vessel or the vehicle, that counts. When humility is absent *in* a ministry, so should we absent ourselves *from* that ministry.

FIVE

The Good Medicine

When we want to be something other than the thing God wants us to be, we must be wanting what, in fact, will not make us happy. Those Divine demands which sound to our natural ears most like those of a despot and least like those of a lover, in fact marshal us where we should want to go if we knew what we wanted.

C. S. Lewis[1]

Imagine yourself, if you will, as a juror. Closing arguments have begun in the trial of a noted drug kingpin. The defense counsel approaches the jury stand where you are seated. He leans over and smiles just a few inches from your face.

"My client doesn't deny pushing millions of dollars' worth of cocaine," he says deliciously. "In fact, he's proud of it. Were it not for his singular effort, ladies and gentlemen, literally thousands of people in this city would today be without a major source of enjoyment. How can you even think of sending my client to prison? He has made many, many people happy. They appreciate what he does for them. In truth, he probably has more followers than the mayor!"

How many of us would buy this argument? Is the defense attorney justified in drawing our attention to the drug-users' apparent happiness (*pleasure* might be a better word)? Does it make a difference that his client enjoys a large and supportive customer base? Would we use the word *loving* to describe the dealer's activity?

In all likelihood this smug narcotics peddler would find little sympathy from us. Most if not all of us would characterize the defense argument as ludicrous. But why? What are our reasons? We would certainly not object to the defendant's claim of a wide following. Nor would we dispute the fact that his actions brought pleasure (fleeting though it may have been) into the lives of his customers. Legalities aside, our prime concern would have to be the dealer's penchant for separating people from reality. Dissociative behavior, however blissful it may seem, is not something a society can afford to promote or exacerbate. Left unchecked it can, and eventually will, erode the foundations of the most stable kingdom.

There is mounting evidence that the Western Church has just such a problem. At almost every turn religious people are being separated from reality. The responsible agency, however, is neither drugs nor those who push them. It is unsound doctrine. As we learned in chapter 1, these alluring but flesh-spun ideas are being dispensed by "side-door" teachers whose sole aim is to "seduce the unstable" (2 Peter 2:14). Their stultifying products are wrapped not in plastic baggies but in attractive dust jackets, CD cases and four-color brochures.

"Popular Christianity parrots the language of New Testament theology," A. W. Tozer declared in *God Tells the Man Who Cares*, "but it accepts the world's opinion of itself."[2] Its proponents lead the children of God away from the light by giving them what they want.

This differs markedly from the good, if sometimes bitter, medicine that is dispensed by the Great Physician. "God is love," John tells us, and everything that proceeds from His heart reflects this (see 1 John 4:16). We do not always get what we want, but we will surely get what is best for us. C. S. Lewis described this process memorably in *Mere Christianity:*

> When I was a child I often had toothache, and I knew that if I went to my mother she would give me something which would deaden the pain for that night and let me get to sleep. But I did not go to my mother—at least, not till the pain became very bad. And the reason I did not go was this. I did not doubt she would give me the aspirin; but I knew she would also do something else. I knew she would take me to the dentist next morning. I could not get what I wanted out of her without getting something more, which I did not want. I wanted immediate relief from pain: but I could not get it without having my teeth set permanently right. And I knew those dentists; I knew they started fiddling about with all sorts of other teeth which had not yet begun to ache. They would not let sleeping dogs lie: if you gave them an inch they took an ell.
>
> Now, if I may put it that way, our Lord is like the dentist. If you give him an inch, he will take an ell.[3]

Constraining Love

Many readers will relate to Lewis' analogy only too well. Some of us may even regard God's dental chair as a second home. We have no doubt that thoroughness is His modus operandi, but we are less certain as to *why* He is so meticulous. The above anecdote covers approach, not motive. God's conscientiousness may be analogous to that of a good dentist, but He fusses over us for reasons that are altogether different. We are not just *a* patient, we are *the* patient. The unfathomable truth is, He loves us.

We are His garden and He intends to maintain us. At times the process will be invasive. A certain amount of pounding and pulling and furrowing goes with the territory. As Lewis noted, a garden will remain distinct from a wilderness "only if someone does all these things to it." But "the very fact that it needs constant weeding and pruning bears witness to [its] glory."[4]

Putting the matter in more relational terms, Lewis asked:

> When we fall in love with a woman, do we cease to care whether she is clean or dirty, fair or foul? Do we not rather then first begin to care? Does any woman regard it as a sign of love in a man that he neither knows nor cares how she is looking?[5]

God's love is so finely focused as to be virtually blind. It sees only the optimum course, the wisest move, the most salutary choice. There may at that moment be a thousand other quite good options, but God is not the least bit interested in them. "What is love," Muggeridge asks, "but a face, instantly recognizable in a sea of faces? A spotlight rather than a panning shot?"[6]

Where we hope to find security in a broad range of possibilities, the broader the better, He knows that all but one of these potential courses will lead us into confusion, temptation, mediocrity or heartache. Rather than view gradations of correctness, God sees the choices before us in black and white (see Psalm 139:23–24; Daniel 2:22; Hebrews 4:12–13). He is ever winnowing the good from the best.

The wonderful thing about God's love, however, is that even if we make a deficient choice and end up on a road we were never intended to take, His divine computer automatically recalculates the optimum course for our lives from this position. The fresh coordinates immediately become the focus of His heart desire for us. God's love, in other words, is always laboring to keep us from the danger of unreality. It brings us at every moment to where we need to be. As Lewis observed in this chapter's opening quote, God's love marshals us where we would go if we truly knew what we wanted.

To take full advantage of God's navigational prowess, we must give ourselves to Him fully. This is not so He might exercise a smothering, despotic control over our lives; it is simply the best of all possible choices. As I explained in one of my earlier books *(The God They Never Knew)*, we choose the things we do on the basis of their intrinsic value. A harmonica is not a Stradivarius, nor will tin ever possess the luster of gold.

As God lovingly and wisely surveys His created universe, He is acutely aware that in order to will our highest good, He must will His *own* highest good. The happiness of all creation hangs dependent on His well-being. So basic is this truth that it is understood even by children. A cute illustration is provided in the following prayer offered up by a little girl:

> Dear God, please take care of my daddy, and my mommy, and my brother and sister, and my doggy, and me. And, oh, please take care of Yourself, God. If anything happens to You, we're gonna be in a big mess.[7]

God recognizes that the intrinsic value of His own being is unsurpassed in the cosmos. As a result He unselfishly requires us to choose Him supremely for our own welfare. If, as God surveyed the universe, He were able to discover something more valuable than Himself, He would, acting in wisdom, require us to choose that end instead.

When an object is perceived or understood by the mind to be intrinsically valuable (valuable in and of itself), we cannot help but choose or refuse it. Put another way, if we choose any object other than that which we have come to understand as possessing intrinsic value, we are making a deficient choice—a *knowingly* deficient choice the Bible calls sin.[8]

If we ask God for bread, He will not give us a stone (see Matthew 7:9), but neither will He guarantee that we will like the taste of His loaf. When He speaks to us, it may not be what we want to hear, but it will always be what needs to be said. Anything less would be unloving.

What the Flesh Wants

As we noted in chapter 3, ministry that caters to the flesh is dangerous in that it leads people away from reality. What we have not yet explored fully is the question of what the flesh wants. Lewis offers some initial thoughts in *The Problem of Pain:*

> What would really satisfy us would be a God who said of any-thing we happened to like doing, "What does it matter so long as they are contented?" We want, in fact, not so much a Father in Heaven as a grandfather in heaven—a senile benevolence who, as they say, "liked to see young people enjoying themselves," and whose plan for the universe was simply that it might be truly said at the end of each day, "a good time was had by all."[9]

This notion is also shared, to one degree or another, by modern-day false teachers. As Peter warned they would, these "slaves of corruption" speak swelling words of vanity and "allure through the lusts of the flesh" (2 Peter 2:18–19, NKJV). They cater to those who would say to Christ, "We will eat our own food and wear our own apparel; only let us be called by your name, to take away our reproach" (Isaiah 4:1, NKJV).

The late positive thinking guru Norman Vincent Peale once said, "The greatest day in any individual's life is when he begins for the first time to realize himself."[10] According to author and psychologist Paul Vitz, it was Peale's Christian rationalization of self-interest that was most responsible for his extraordinary popularity. Citing chapter titles like "How to Create Your Own Happiness" and "How to Draw upon that Higher Power," Vitz warned that Peale's message "reduces God to a useful servant of the individual in his quest for personal goals."[11]

That which is contrary to the Spirit is contrary to reality. The Spirit says, "This world is not your home. You are just a pilgrim passing through." The flesh says, "Let's camp!" The Spirit says, "Die to yourself that you might live." The flesh says, "Live it up now because you're going to die!"

This emphasis on the tangible and immediate is reminiscent of the children of Israel who, tiring of heavenly manna, "tested God in their heart by asking for the food of their fancy" (Psalm 78:18, NKJV). "Can God prepare a table in the wilderness?" they asked cynically. "Can He provide meat for His people?" (verses 19–20, NKJV).

As John Wright Follette pointed out, "It is not always a question: 'Is God able?' but, 'Is it God's will and purpose?'"[12] If we press our interests too hard, God just might grant them (see Psalm 78:29). While this may appear at first to be a divine capitulation, it is actually the toughest kind of love. Just as mothers sometimes let insistent children learn that eating too much apple pie will produce a stomachache, so God allows us to experience the emotional blisters that come from chasing ephemeral pleasures.

We are all, in a sense, like thirsty desert wanderers. It is natural for us to jump at the first "sighting" of desperately needed water. But we are wise not to run after it long. We will notice that the water we seek to quench our thirst is keeping its fair distance, no matter how much ground we cover. It is a mirage, and rushing after it will only exacerbate our thirst.

Unfortunately some of our emotional lives have been cultivated for so long that they are tremblingly alive to the things of the world. This has made us an attractive habitation for sin's extended family. We continue with ministry as usual because irresponsible shepherds and deceitful hearts have blinded us to the true nature of our soul's "guests." Our only hope of eradicating this infestation is to gain enlightenment through the words of a godly truth-teller, or to see ourselves in the mirror of sudden provocation. As Lewis reminded us:

If there are rats in the cellar you are most likely to see them if you go in very suddenly. But the suddenness does not create the rats: it only prevents them from hiding. In the same way the suddenness of the provocation does not make me an ill-tempered man: it only shows me what an ill-tempered man I am.[13]

The Plague and the Cross

One method that will *not* bring us deliverance from ourselves or the world is abstinence. Jesus said that "unless a grain of wheat falls into the ground and dies, it remains alone" (John 12:24, NKJV). The individual who chooses to hold on and resist the world through abstinence, rather than abiding, is fighting a losing battle. We are simply too ill-equipped to conquer sin on our own. In the words of the great Chinese Bible teacher Watchman Nee:

> Abstinence is merely worldly. Yet how many earnest Christians are forsaking all sorts of worldly pleasures in the hope thereby of being delivered out of the world! You can build yourself a hermit's hut in some remote spot and think to escape the world by retiring there, but the world will follow you. . . . It will dog your footsteps and find you no matter where you hide. Our deliverance from the world begins, not with our giving up this or that, but with our seeing, as with God's eyes, that it is a world under sentence of death.[14]

God will deliver us from our nemeses, but only on His terms. He is not interested in halfway measures. He refuses to accept patients who want freedom from their besetting condition but sniff at the idea of ongoing relationship. There can be no rescue without reformation. As Lewis reminded us, it is a hard bargain but one well worth making:

> When a man turns to Christ and seems to be getting on pretty well (in the sense that some of his bad habits are now corrected),

72

he often feels that it would now be natural if things went fairly smoothly. When troubles come along—illnesses, money troubles, new kinds of temptation—he is disappointed. These things, he feels, might have been necessary to rouse him and make him repentant in his bad old days; but why now? Because God is forcing him on, or up, to a higher level: putting him into situations where he will have to be very much braver, or more patient, or more loving, than he ever dreamed of being before. It seems to us all unnecessary: but that is because we have not yet had the slightest notion of the tremendous thing he means to make of us.[15]

Several years ago I was approached by a young man caught in the grip of an intense inner struggle. Jerry was blessed with a whip-cracking intellect that made him an intense and engaging conversationalist. I also discovered that he had been brought up in a Christian home and was well-versed in doctrine. Unfortunately these qualities only seemed to feed his spiritual unrest. After I spent several days trying to isolate the root of Jerry's growing discomfort, the Lord provided an answer through a most unexpected source.

At the time of these counseling sessions, I had been reading Albert Camus' classic novel about a deadly plague that ravaged the Algerian port city of Oran. Near the end of this deeply moving story, Camus describes the ordeal of a priest who contracts the disease after working tirelessly as a volunteer in the overloaded hospital. He is stricken at a time when, by all appearances, the epidemic had passed. The account of his struggle to prevent the plague from claiming him as one of its final victims is a poignant drama.

The next time I sat down with my young friend, I knew what to say.

"Jerry," I began, "you're resisting the Divine Plague. You've been fighting tenaciously to hang onto your life, and God wants you to let go. He wants you to succumb. He wants you to die! As long as you retain control of your life, He cannot accomplish His purposes."

Finally the dam in Jerry's heart broke, and the years of resistance flowed out in a torrent of tears.

This is God's way. Until we are prepared to yield to Him completely, He will faithfully trouble us. That is why He warned people to count the cost before becoming Christians. As the great Christian writer George MacDonald pointed out, "God is easy to please, but hard to satisfy."[16] His relentless manner was captured eloquently by Muggeridge in *Jesus Rediscovered:*

> God comes padding after me like a Hound of Heaven. His shadow falls over all my little picnics in the sunshine, chilling the air, draining viands of their flavor, talk of its sparkle, desire of its zest. . . . One shivers as the divine beast of prey gets ready for the final spring; as the shadow lengthens, reducing to infinite triviality all mortal hopes and desires.[17]

Not yielding up to God what is rightfully His amounts to sacrilegious theft. But we cling to our lives because we are not yet convinced that God's medicine is good. We are worried that He will go too far, that there will soon be nothing left of us. We often try to conclude the matter like the young lad who was overheard praying, "Lord, If You can't make me a better boy, don't worry about it. I'm having a real good time like I am."

And His methods are painful. No sooner are we pricked by illness or misunderstanding than we scurry off to the comforting arms of mercy-minded friends and ministers. But we must be wary, for as Follette warned us, "Self-pity, a moist-eyed creature, lurks there." As long as we "linger and are willing to be coddled by her, just so long [we] will hinder God and lose out in overcoming."[18]

God is not attempting to strip away our dreams and ambitions altogether. He is merely trying to encourage us toward that which will really satisfy. He encourages those "who hunger and thirst for righteousness" that "they will be filled" (Matthew 5:6). We hear the voice of God booming across the desert,

"Come, all you who are thirsty, come to the waters" (Isaiah 55:1). The man who "loses" his life does not die in the desert chasing mirages; he discovers a new inner oasis. "Whoever drinks the water I give him will never thirst," Jesus said. "Indeed, the water I give him will become in him a spring of water welling up to eternal life" (John 4:14).

Those who release themselves utterly into the hands of God will discover a sense of abandonment to the things that previously occupied their hearts. It is at once a feeling of near-weightless relief and a sense of being borne up into the heavenlies, where life suddenly takes on a brand-new perspective. We are freed from the burden of managing our own affairs that we might give attention to the King's business. As Lewis observed:

> The Christian way is different: harder and easier. Christ says, "Give Me all. I don't want so much of your time and so much of your money and so much of your work: I want you. I have not come to torment your natural self, but to kill it."[19]

I once received a letter from a student begging me to instruct him on how he might die to himself. He was more than willing. Indeed he was almost obsessed with the need to terminate his self-interest. He just did not know how to go about it.

My answer was, "Don't do it! Don't try to set up your own execution." Many Christians misinterpret Jesus' admonition to "take up your cross" as a signal to begin immediate cross-building. Although Jesus did instruct us to bear up the instrument of our deaths, He never suggested that we attempt spiritual self-execution. As Follette explained in his devotional classic *Broken Bread:*

> You will have to interpret your own cross, for yours is not like anyone else's. It will be a cross fitting your whole concept and disposition, and more than that, your *will*. Whatever you are *in your will*, determines your cross. What may be a cross to you may

seem like a joy-ride to another. It is that which will crucify the *I* in you that will determine your cross. . . .[20]

Why can't we build our own crosses? Simply because the kind we build do not get the job done. They are too plush and invariably leave us very much alive. Twenty-first-century models, replete with extra padding, an exercise bike and remote control television, are especially ineffective. To help ease the pain, if there is any, sympathetic friends are encouraged to pass up a sponge filled with cappuccino or Perrier. Within a few days the disciple dismounts his cross and begins to share on the resurrection life—of which he knows nothing, owing to the fact that he never died in the first place!

If we wait on the Lord, He will, Master Craftsman that He is, fashion a cross for us that will accomplish its purpose. Its design, rather than allowing us to repose in style, will slay us. He knows what it will take to bring us to our end. As Fénelon said:

> He disillusions us with ourselves by the experience of our weakness and our corruption, in an infinite number of failures; and yet, even then when He seems to overwhelm us, it is for our good; it is to spare us from the harm which we would do to ourselves. What we weep for would have made us weep eternally. What we believe to have been lost was lost when we thought we had it.[21]

False Prophets and Negligent Healers

Not all ministries bear the good medicine trademark. Indeed some popularity hounds see it as the kiss of death. Nobody generates a following by peddling castor oil or performing root canals. Many modern writers and preachers acknowledge the necessity of such things but limit their "healing" practices to vitamins and Band-Aids. They prefer to be liked rather than be truly helpful.

These attitudes are nothing new. When King Ahab contemplated going to battle against the king of Aram, he solicited the assistance of Jehoshaphat, king of Judah. The latter, while expressing a willingness to participate in the venture, advised Ahab to "first seek the counsel of the LORD" (1 Kings 22:5). Agreeing to these terms, the king of Israel assembled about four hundred prophets and put forth a single question: "Shall I go to war against Ramoth Gilead, or shall I refrain?" Not surprisingly the consensus was positive. "Go," they answered, "for the Lord will give it into the king's hand" (verse 6). Jehoshaphat, however, was troubled. There was something about these prophets that rang false. He asked, "Is there not a prophet of the Lord here whom we can inquire of?" (verse 7).

Ahab's response was revealing—almost humorous in a perverse sense. "There is still one man through whom we can inquire of the LORD," he told Jehoshaphat, "but I hate him because he never prophesies anything good about me, but always bad" (verse 8). Startled by this comment, the king of Judah pressed Ahab to bring Micaiah the prophet before the court.

When the king's messenger arrived at the prophet's residence, he offered a piece of friendly advice. "Look, as one man the other prophets are predicting success for the king. Let your word agree with theirs, and speak favorably" (verse 13). Micaiah, however, was not one to be swayed so easily. He was a truth-teller, a deliverer of the hard but authentic word. He alone among the prophets bore the trademark of heaven. He alone rose above his natural desire to be thought of in positive terms.

In the end Micaiah's words proved to be as accurate, and dire, as Ahab had feared. After the evil king was slain in his chariot by a random arrow, his blood was licked up by dogs.

Jeremiah, too, lamented over the bad medicine and false assurances dispensed by the reigning religious establishment:

> "From the least to the greatest,
> all are greedy for gain;

> prophets and priests alike,
> all practice deceit.
> They dress the wound of my people
> as though it were not serious.
> 'Peace, peace,' they say,
> when there is no peace."
>
> Jeremiah 6:13–14

The tendency to minimize corporate sin for personal gain is lambasted by God in Ezekiel 34. In this instance the problem is not prophets and priests who dress wounds "as though [they] were not serious," but shepherds who "have not strengthened the weak or healed the sick or bound up the injured" (verse 4). Like all self-interested ministers, they "cared for themselves rather than for [God's] flock" (verse 8).

Sadly this dismal performance is a recurring theme throughout Scripture (see Judges 17; 2 Kings 21:9; Isaiah 56:11; Jeremiah 23:2, 9–11; 50:6; Ezekiel 13; Micah 3:5–12; Zephaniah 3:4; Zechariah 11:17; Matthew 7:15; John 10:12; Titus 1:10–11; 2 Peter 2:1–3; and all of Jude). In the vast majority of these cases, bad medicine ministers damaged God's flock by filling them with false hopes (see Jeremiah 23:16–17) and failing to expose sin (see Lamentations 2:14). The situation is little changed today.

It would be wrong, however, to place the blame solely on weak and deceitful spiritual leaders. If they have found success in false assurances and "great swelling words," it is only because there is a ready market. Samuels, Nathans and Micaiahs are out there; we are just not interested in their message. In the words of Jeremiah 5:30–31:

> "A horrible and shocking thing
> has happened in the land:
> The prophets prophesy lies,
> the priests rule by their own authority,
> and my people love it this way."

So prevalent is this tendency to minimize (or rationalize) sin that penetrating words are often classified as judgmental and treated with the same disdain as racial epithets. Some Christians are actually convinced that messages on holiness are a form of legalism.

I can still remember the day my father returned home with just such a story. The conveners of a large charismatic convention in the Pacific Northwest had apparently objected to a teaching on holiness he had delivered in one of the plenary sessions. Although the word had caused God's convicting presence to fall in a powerful way, the men on the platform were decidedly unhappy. They had been counting on a more celebratory environment. After my father concluded his message and sat down, the auditorium went momentarily silent. Nobody said a word as the Spirit began to expose the sinful condition of people's hearts.

It was all too much for the men seated behind the podium. One gentleman promptly rose to his feet and grabbed the microphone. "I'd like you all to stand," he said breathlessly, "and join me in proclaiming the grace of God."

For the next several minutes he assumed the role of a yell-leader, shouting out the word "Grace!" and waiting for the audience to respond. This was then followed by a collective chant of "Liberty, liberty!"

The leaders of this meeting did not want a message on holiness, which they mistakenly assumed would bring God's people into bondage, but a word of reassurance, a song of optimism. In their dismissal of truth, however, they became "servants of corruption;" proclaiming liberty to others while they themselves remained captive to fleshly interests (see 2 Peter 2:19, KJV). The only difference between these leaders and the false shepherds mentioned in Jeremiah 6 is that they declared, "Grace, grace," rather than "Peace, peace."

Nor was this the only time my father witnessed human interference with the Great Physician's work. A second incident, equally memorable, occurred during a counseling session with the brilliant aeronautical engineer Bill Lear (whose accomplishments include the Lear Executive Jet).

My father had worked for Lear in the late 1950s as his corporate general manager. Despite the latter's reputation as a hard-living eccentric, my father retained a fondness for him. Years after leaving Lear's employ, my father was prompted by the Lord to call Bill. Although the two had not spoken for many years, he still knew how to reach his home in Reno, Nevada.

Bill Lear answered the phone.

"Bill, this is George Otis. I know this may sound odd, but the Lord placed you on my heart this morning. I just had to call and find out what's happening in your life. God's thinking about you, Bill."

There was a long silence on the other end of the line.

"It's good to hear from you," Lear said tersely. "But could you call me back in ten or fifteen minutes?"

The second time Bill's voice sounded brighter.

"I need to share something with you, George. Something amazing. When you called a few minutes ago, I was sitting at my desk preparing to take my own life. I haven't been well and I thought my revolver was the answer."

As the two men continued their conversation, Bill asked my father if he could possibly come up to Reno. He agreed, and several days later was sitting across from his old boss in the Lears' living room. They were joined by Joy Dawson, a widely known Bible teacher, and Bill's wife, Moira.

Not knowing how much longer Bill would live, the two ministers seized the occasion to make a clear presentation of the Gospel. God would deliver him, but only if there was no whitewashing of sin.

It proved to be a tough session. As Joy pressed Bill to see the gravity of his sin and repent in a very specific manner, Moira became greatly agitated. Putting her arm around her husband, she exclaimed, "He's not that bad. He's just not all that bad."

While this response may appear a loyal and loving act, it was, in fact, just the opposite. Moira Lear had become, perhaps unwittingly, a serious obstacle to Bill on his route to deliverance. Like all well-intentioned but false words, "they did not expose [his] sin to ward off [his] captivity" (Lamentations 2:14).

Fortunately Bill Lear pressed into God and was converted. He died shortly thereafter.

God's Word is not filled with disclaimers or apologies. He means what He says, and He says what needs to be said. If we are to represent accurately His heart and interests, we must do likewise. We should speak in love, but it must be the truth (see Ephesians 4:15). Anything less is bad medicine.

Avoiding the Dangers of New Egypt

Good medicine is not always what it seems. To accomplish His purposes, God sometimes uses tools and concepts that were not part of His original intention for us. Chief among these are illness and death. Although they work, they are harsh to the system—a characteristic that often causes them to be seen as the reason for our problem rather than the cure.

Wandering is another of these strange medicines. Since God is always talking about lighting our paths (see Psalm 119:105) and making them straight (see Hebrews 12:13), we can hardly appreciate that He would lead us in circles. But wandering is not so much about detour as it is about delay. Sometimes God slows our pace that He might divest us of a flawed mentality or worldview. This, according to mission pastor Ruth Ruibal, is precisely what He did with the Hebrews in Sinai. If they had been allowed to carry their old attitudes and habit patterns directly into the Promised Land, it would almost certainly have become New Egypt.

In similar fashion, godly leaders do not rush new converts into positions of authority. Their young and talented disciples often chafe at this delay (and other attendant restrictions), but the wait is invariably good and loving medicine. "Character," it has been said, "is a victory, not a gift."[22] It is something to be contended for rather than received as a birthright. God's gift to us is the daily opportunity to embrace His will with ours.

SIX

THE FRESH BREAD

*The Christian must not allow himself to be entrapped by cur-
rent vogues in religion, and above all he must never go to the
world for his message.*

A. W. Tozer[1]

As we traverse this cavernous world strewn with empty platitudes, stale routines and fetching eye candy, there is a growing hunger for that which is genuine and substantial. This
yearning is found not only in the hearts of the non-religious,
where it might be expected, but also among those who pro-
fess a relationship with God. Both have approached truth's
table only to find it wanting. (One day it is piled with plastic
display food; on another it is littered with the crumbs of yesterday's leftovers.) So the search continues—in the classroom,
in the chat room, in the chapel—for a true meal, for victuals
that will curb the insistent hunger pangs of the soul.

A loaf of bread, the Walrus said,
Is what we chiefly need.[2]

So spoke the chief character in Lewis Carroll's absurd 1872 poem "The Walrus and the Carpenter." And the portly marine gentleman would still draw a hearty *Amen!*

Bread is exactly what God offers us. And it is "the true bread from heaven" (John 6:32), the One who declared, "I am the bread of life. He who comes to me will never go hungry" (verse 35). It is Jesus the satisfier.

The Bread of heaven is the Word of God in expression. He is not only true, He is fresh and creative. He satisfies continually. Everything that comes out of His mouth bears truth and stimulates life. It is a force beyond scope or measure.

God promises to do a *new thing* (Isaiah 43:19) and *make everything new* (Revelation 21:5). Because His *mercies are new* every morning (Lamentations 3:23), He offers to make a *new covenant* (Jeremiah 31:31; Hebrews 8:8) and call us by a *new name* (Isaiah 62:2). As we put on the *new man* (Ephesians 4:24, KJV), He puts a *new song* in our mouths (Psalm 40:3). He gives us a *new heart* and a *new spirit* (Ezekiel 18:31; 36:26), followed by *new fruit* and *new wine* (Ezekiel 47:12; John 2:10). Finally, when time has run its course, He will make a *new heaven* and a *new earth* (Isaiah 65:17; Revelation 21:1).

Apart from God's holiness and selfless and far-reaching love, it is His creativity that stands out as perhaps His most dominant characteristic. God is, and always has been, a creator. Creativity is His nature, His very essence. It is impossible for Him to author or deliver ministry that is worn, vapid, stale or routine.

Routines as Placeholders

Those who gravitate to routines and certain rituals do so out of convenience. They lean on them as they would on a steady handrail, a helpful outline or a ready chauffeur. They like the fact that routines help them remember things without taxing their energy. They laud their ability to provide shelter from the buffeting winds of change.

Spiritual storm-chasers, on the other hand, view these apparent advantages as unhealthy temptations, if not overt obstacles, on the road to truth. Their supreme desire is to acquire revelation that will effect change—in their own lives and in the world around them. To reach this goal they must first cast off the blanket of sameness.

Both groups agree on one thing: Routines are boring and predictable. Indeed they are boring precisely *because* they are predictable. Their metronomic cadence allows us to safely "check out" of conversations, work or worship. Their role is to maintain. They are placeholders rather than conveyors.

Religious routines and rituals can offer a "form of godliness" (see 2 Timothy 3:5), but it will be sanitized of any real personality and power. Those who pursue such religion are either unsure whether God exists or they are unwilling to find out. Like the unfortunate souls described in Matthew 7:21–23, they have religion but no relationship. Their rituals become a placeholder for an absent God.

"I think it is this deep-seated notion that God is absent," Tozer once said, "that makes so many of our church services so insufferably dull."[3] To dismiss this statement as pious zeal is to miss the point. It is only a small step from boredom to disillusionment. And the progression from there is to self-pity and, ultimately, to chaos.

"Is not life a hundred times too short for us to bore ourselves?"[4] Nietzsche once asked. How long can we afford to eat bread that is neither tasty nor nourishing? How often can we go to church without being stimulated by a new thought or a fresh revelation?[5]

A. W. Tozer, himself a long-time Alliance pastor, lamented the qualitative deterioration of our services:

> In the majority of our meetings there is scarcely a trace of reverent thought, no recognition of the unity of the body, little sense

of divine Presence, no moment of stillness, no solemnity, no wonder, no holy fear. But so often there is a dull or a breezy song leader full of awkward jokes, as well as a chairman announcing each "number" with the old radio continuity patter in an effort to make everything hang together.[6]

"Even before the music begins," American novelist Henry Miller wrote in *Tropic of Cancer,* "there is that bored look on people's faces."[7] Although he spoke of secular concerts, he might well have described Christian worship. In many of our services, worship has become guided and predictable, an autonomic response rather than a thoughtful gesture. Some songs are little more than rote drills. They are what Rex Humbard calls "7–11 worship": singing seven words, eleven times.

This descent into shallow and repetitive worship is well illustrated in the following amusing but all too familiar story submitted by my dear friend and colleague Jeff Hastings.

An old farmer went to the city one weekend and attended the big city church. When he came home, his wife asked him what he thought.

"Well," said the farmer, "it was good. But they did something different. They sang praise choruses instead of hymns."

"Praise choruses?" said his wife. "What are those?"

"Oh, they're O.K. They're sort of like hymns, only different."

"What's the difference?"

The farmer said, "Well, it's like this. If I were to say to you, 'Martha, the cows are in the corn,' well, that would be a hymn. But if I were to say to you,

Martha, Martha, Martha,
Oh, *Martha, Martha, Martha,*
The cows, the big cows, the brown cows, the black cows,
the white cows, the black and white cows,
the *cows, cows, cows* are in the corn,
are in the corn, are in the corn, are in the corn,
the *corn, corn, corn,*

and then if I were to repeat the whole thing two or three times—well, that would be a praise chorus."

As humorous as this story is, it is not that far removed from reality. Some years ago I spoke at a church camp in the mountains. During the worship time leading up to my teaching, the gravity of the situation hit me full-force. Lifting their voices, the campers sang a refrain that went something like this:

> Just as one and one are two,
> and two and two are four,
> Blink your eyes and turn around
> and He'll be yours forevermore.

How far removed this is from the rich, expressive worship that sprang from the hearts of Miriam and David! How unlike the authoritative pronouncements of Isaiah, Jeremiah or Ezekiel. Yet it is just the sort of vague, gooey, abstract teaching that many Christians seem to latch onto these days.

But that youth camp chorus is no less articulate than the popular (and endlessly repeating) charismatic refrain "Yes, Lord, yes, Lord, yes, yes, Lord." We have become like the people of Isaiah's day who were "ever hearing, but never understanding" (see Isaiah 6:9). The question is, Why? Does not Scripture admonish us to "sing praises with understanding" (Psalm 47:7, NKJV)? And are we not to "sing to [the LORD] a *new* song" (Psalm 33:3, emphasis added; Isaiah 42:10)?

If we cannot sing a new song, it is because God has not put one into our mouths (see Psalm 40:3). True celebration can only follow liberation (see Exodus 15; Psalm 30) or revelation (see Revelation 5:9; 14:3). If we know of such things, how often do they guide our worship, whether corporate or private? If we expect our pastors to wait on God for fresh bread, why do we have no similar expectation of our worship leaders? How can worship be truly dynamic when those who lead it do nothing more than reach into a box of overhead transparencies?

We have songleaders but we need psalmists. We have speakers but we need prophets. We have leaders but we need wise men. As Os Guinness reminds us:

> Due to the twin factors of the presence of sin and the passing of time, no personal relationship or spiritual experience is self-perpetuating. Each must be nourished, sustained, and fanned into flame again and again or it will die. Not even spiritual revivals last. The natural course of entropy in things personal and spiritual is toward decline and death, or toward the atrophying ugliness that such words as formalizing and routinizing aim to convey. With repetition the extraordinary becomes ordinary and the revolutionary routine. Whereas "Christ" is free and fresh, "Christianity" is often formal and dead—or worse.[8]

What Is Creative?

C. S. Lewis once noted in an essay on Christianity and literature that none of our spirituality is creative in the sense of being original.[9] Instead we are called to replicate, or reflect, something more ancient and profound. This is also the message of an earlier preacher (probably Solomon) who observed in Ecclesiastes 1:10:

> Is there anything of which one can say,
> "Look! This is something new"?
> It was here already, long ago;
> it was here before our time.

Dr. Paul Vitz, whom we met in chapter 5, elaborates on this theme in his insightful book *Psychology as Religion:*

> For a Christian, all creativity has its origin in God. And to claim that an individual human is really creative is either silly or blasphemous. A person can express his individual capacity in a cre-

ative fashion only by aligning himself with God's will. Real creativity requires a soul cooperating with God—a soul who becomes God's loving agent in all its activity however mundane. There is certainly no Christian basis for the massive egos so common in the modern artist.[10]

Vitz adds his belief that "a true Christian artist or writer should never strive for creativity *per se* but instead should try to embody some reflection of eternal beauty and wisdom."[11] True creativity is transformative. It gives birth to new insights and reordered priorities. It inspires men and women to look beyond themselves.

Many ministers get hung up on packaging when God is focused on content. They worry about preparing outlines while God is looking for prepared hearts. In their headlong pursuit of excellence, they forget that creative ministry is not about obsessing over details but about making disciples. While delivery is not unimportant, it means nothing if it fails to inspire change. God is interested in results that last.

God's Spirit is dynamic. If there is a desire for growth, His creativity provides spiritual food; if there is a need for guidance, He reveals the next step; if there is a problem, His creativity offers a way out. If God has inspired a message or ministry, changed lives and circumstances will be the inevitable result.

Today we send students off to schools of creative ministry, but the results are often anything but creative. Indeed, states Vitz, "Creative [potential] programs have become schools for inordinate pride."[12] Our techniques merely ape those of the world, and all too often fail to change or transform the lives of our audience.

Some time back I was asked by a group of Christian young people what I thought about a particular Christian rock band. Did I approve of their performance? Did I agree with their approach to ministry? After thinking about the question for a moment, I responded, "I really can't answer you. I have never sat under their ministry, if indeed that's what it is. But I *can* tell you how to discern the situation for yourself. The secret has nothing to do with the decibel level or beat of their music. It has everything to do with the hearts and lives of their listeners. Are they changed? Is there growth of character? If so, then the band's ministry is truly creative—and I'm all for it."

The term *Christian entertainment* has entered our vocabulary of late. But what exactly is it? I know what entertainment is, and I know what Christians are, but what is Christian entertainment? Is it simply a matter of adding God words to our lyrics? Does it apply if the performer professes faith in Christ? What if these elements are missing? Does this make the performance unchristian and inappropriate?

There is no doubt that God has created us with a capacity, and perhaps even a need, to be entertained. Our hearts are lifted by good music and well-crafted literature. They are healed through clean humor. Sports, too, can provide a wholesome diversion (although this is not always the case). God has no problem with Christians being entertained or providing entertainment for others. But entertainment is not ministry, and entertainers are not ministers. The blurring of this distinction is one of the chief concerns within Christendom today.

It is also worth pointing out that the entertainment industry has grown into a multibillion dollar industry largely because multitudes are hurting and lonely. People are in pain and trying to cover that pain. But what would happen to the entertainment industry if God's people began to minister faithfully the creative life of Christ to people in need of that ministry? It is something to think about.

The world needs fresh bread, but the Church needs it first. We cannot offer to others what we do not have ourselves. There is a desperate hunger growing that can be filled only with godly content and eternal truth. Slick plastic wrappers will not do the job. Is there newness in our message or ministry? Is there power to bring about change? If not, we must go back to the bakery.

God is not interested in entertainment that takes the guise of ministry. This is why Jesus, after spending just 33 years on earth, was able to say to His Father, "I have finished the work which You have given Me to do" (John 17:4, NKJV). He accomplished this remarkable feat, according to J. Oswald Sanders, by spending time on things that mattered.[13] He did not walk around entertaining people; He went about changing people. He met their deepest needs.

And so must we.

We must take care, in the words of Alexander Solzhenitsyn, that we not "overheat [ourselves] with ephemeral concerns and boil dry."[14] It is only as we consume, and are consumed with, the true Bread of Life that we will finally understand true creativity.

Butter for the Royal Slice of Bread

Truly creative ministers will always capture two things: difficult concepts and the attention of an audience. Nobody did this better than the great Oxford scholar C. S. Lewis. Although he possessed formidable academic credentials and tackled thorny and complex subjects (ranging from the nature of hell to the problem of pain), he never allowed his erudition to stumble the common man. Like the learned Paul, he resolved to put aside "eloquence [and] superior wisdom" (1 Corinthians 2:1) so that his works would remain ever accessible. As a consequence Lewis went on to become one of the world's most beloved and bestselling authors.

Creative ministry brings joy and enlightenment to children as well as to scholars. Its aim is to reveal secrets, not simply to discover them. It is about helping people complete the puzzle of life. Godly servants go about this business gently, often using parables and metaphors to stimulate thoughtful observation. Fleshly performers, on the other hand, try to capture attention through intimidation (often pressing educational credentials into service) or emotional manipulation.

This latter tactic is particularly effective since modern audiences are rarely satisfied with basic meals or unembroidered preaching. Like youngsters at an auntie's dinner table, they are eager for something extra—a garnish, a dessert, a topping.

A. A. Milne of Winnie the Pooh fame alludes generically to this inclination in his 1924 book *When We Were Very Young:*

> The Queen asked
> The Dairymaid,
> 'Could we have some butter for
> The Royal slice of bread?'[15]

If the royal slice of bread is the Word and revelation of God, the butter is whatever we add to make it more tasty. There is no sin in presenting truth in a creative fashion, but some toppings and seasonings fail to complement God's underlying entrée. They either dull it with their tastelessness or are so intensely flavored as to overwhelm and conceal.

In practice this detraction can involve anything from a singer's stage gyrations to a pastor's insipid humor. It has also been known to occur through celebrity showcasing and culture-centric writing or performances. (This latter example is not intended to suggest that God's truth cannot be conveyed through varied and unique cultural expressions. Indeed cultures are His handiwork on display, a character-revealing extravagance. Unless a particular expression becomes inward-looking, it is the perfect vehicle for His sovereign revelation.)

Windbags and Wineskins

Preaching styles and techniques are undoubtedly the most common form of spiritual "butter." Whether they actually enhance the taste of royal bread is another matter. Many people clearly think so. Judging by the marked popularity of some of today's more idiosyncratic and flamboyant ministers, it can at least be said that methods are useful in capturing the attention of an audience.

But we may not want to hand out certificates of authenticity just yet. These preachers have met only the first standard of creative communication. They have proven they can grab the minds of listeners—but what are they saying? What kind of content lies behind their sweating brows, supercharged stories and flowing superlatives? Energy is not anointing, nor is eloquence substance.

Speakers who say nothing with great intensity are like "clouds carried by a tempest" (2 Peter 2:17, NKJV). They are masters of the well-inflected phrase but failures at transmitting life-giving truth. In the end their ability to speak "great swelling words of emptiness" (verse 18) qualifies them only as highly skilled windbags.

The good news is that true seekers will eventually recognize they are being shortchanged. This epiphany may come suddenly, perhaps during the course of an animated but otherwise hollow sermon, or as part of a process, in which they finally realize they are not gaining any spiritual weight. Either way the ministry relationship that once engendered excitement and respect begins to elicit disappointment and boredom. With stale bread the order of the day, the preacher's sermons now seem interminable. In the words of J. G. Saxe, "He says a thousand pleasant things— But never says 'Adieu.'"[16]

And it is not just preaching getting old these days. Entropy is also taking a toll on our ministry systems and methodologies. Although this process is not new, and may even be said to be the natural course of things, it is leading us in a decidedly unpleasant direction. Unless it is countered by fresh creativity, our organizations and tactics will degenerate into irrelevance.

Our first response must be to acknowledge the need for change. If we think our structures are impervious to the hidden icebergs of time and tradition, then we are no wiser than the captain of the Titanic. Systemic problems exist, and they will not disappear merely because we cover them with daring new ideas. As Jesus told John's disciples in Matthew 9:16–17:

> "No one sews a patch of unshrunk cloth on an old garment, for the patch will pull away from the garment, making the tear worse. Neither do men pour new wine into old wineskins. If they do, the skins will burst, the wine will run out and the wineskins will be ruined. No, they pour new wine into new wineskins, and both are preserved."

While I will have more to say on this subject in chapter 8, the point for the moment is that new ideas should not be forced into old structures or systems. The latter must be allowed to change along with the former. While this may sound easy, it is not. There is great inertia in organized religion (not to mention in our own lives). Our inclination is to retain the familiar for as long as possible. As a consequence some ministry structures have grown so old they must be preserved by chemists using industrial-strength formaldehyde.

The opposite problem—putting old ideas into new wineskins—is also common today. Ministry packages look and sound great, but there is nothing new or life-changing inside. This is analogous to the computer-maker who designs a stunning case but ends up losing market share because the internal processor is based on decade-old (translate: slow) technology. Other examples include fancy restaurants with bad food or substandard service, and made-up actresses whose natural beauty and character are waning. The solution, as Jesus said, is to "pour new wine into new wineskins" so that "both are preserved."

Many ministries that regard themselves as creative are anything but. Not only is their message flat and tasteless, but their packages are borrowed from a dead and dying system. The results of this "creativity" range from managed ("user-friendly") church services to outlandishly garbed Christian rock groups throwing New Testaments off a platform. Instead of availing themselves of the most imaginative and resourceful personality in the universe, these ministers rely on their own limited devices. Where they could give us the painter of rainbows, we are confronted instead with amateur cartoonists.

As the following passages indicate, God has a keen interest in creative packaging. If we will allow His Spirit to fill and direct us, He will give us the ability to produce songs, sermons and sanctuaries whose quality and originality far exceed anything the world might tempt us to mimic.

> The LORD said to Moses, "See, I have chosen Bezalel son of Uri, the son of Hur, of the tribe of Judah, and *I have filled him with the Spirit of God, with skill, ability and knowledge in all kinds of crafts*—to make artistic designs for work in gold, silver and bronze, to cut and set stones, to work in wood, and to engage in all kinds of craftsmanship. Moreover, I have appointed Oholiab son of Ahisamach, of the tribe of Dan, to help him. Also *I have given skill to all the craftsmen* to make everything I have commanded you. . . ."
>
> Exodus 31:1–6, emphasis added

> The musicians Heman, Asaph and Ethan were to sound the bronze cymbals; Zechariah, Aziel, Shemiramoth, Jehiel, Unni, Eliab, Maaseiah and Benaiah were to play the lyres according to *alamoth* [probably a musical term], and Mattithiah, Eliphelehu, Mikneiah, Obed-Edom, Jeiel and Azaziah were to play the harps, directing according to *sheminith* [probably a musical term]. Kenaniah the head Levite was in charge of the singing; that was his responsibility because *he was skillful at it.*
>
> 1 Chronicles 15:19–22, emphasis added

Interpreting Reality

In August 1996 a ministry research assignment allowed me to glimpse a very different creativity in Nevada's remote Black Rock Desert. I had traveled to this ancient playa to document a burgeoning, techno-pagan festival known as The Burning Man. The event, held every year over Labor Day weekend, is dedicated to transforming the vast alkali flatland into what one reveler called "a temporary autonomous zone at the edge of eternity."

For thousands of soul-seared participants, the "zone" represents an opportunity to shed one's clothes, trance-dance and exchange idols; to others it is simply a creative palette on which to display bizarre art forms. Although many try to label the event—it has been called everything from a "human petri dish" to a "sandblasting of the soul"—this task is as daunting as the environment.

"We built a city of fantasy up from flat clay nothingness," one veteran pilgrim exulted. "We dissolve boundaries and churn the mind." But the glitter and whimsy of this idealistic and ephemeral community exist only for a few late summer days. After that the sounds and images are carried away by dust devils.

Hovering over the center of this sprawling desert camp is the Man himself—an elaborate, forty-foot-tall timber giant. Wrapped in wax-soaked burlap and studded with Roman candles, he serves as a vivid metaphor of the pilgrims' smoldering alienation. Ritually torched on the event's final night, this plywood-boned, neon-veined pyrotechnic wonder is offered as a modern-day religious or philosophical icon.

Those who make the yearly pilgrimage to Black Rock—an eclectic crowd of neopagans, media bohemians and some of the world's top computer animators—are in no mood for rules. Tired of the oppressive hamster wheel of life, they come to cast off restraint. The results include bizarre art displays (ranging from a 75-foot-high wall of pianos to a Winnebago pirate ship); attention-grabbing theme camps (including McSatan's Bistro and the dusk-to-dawn Heathen Drumming Circle); and eye- (and ear-) popping alternative music performances.

"Burning Man brings up ancient feelings inside me," one festival insider shared with an online newsgroup I monitor. "I believe my ancestors felt them right before a war. Flags whipping in the wind, food cooking over gigantic fires, camaraderie, danger, excitement, meeting old friends . . . the sense that we could die today."

"This is millennial stuff, folks," added another soul-stirred participant eager to discover new wineskins:

> I am reminded of the Maya Indians, who at the end of their calendrical cycles took out their pots and jewelry and broke them or threw them into a sacred well. They did this to purify themselves, to start fresh. We as a society so need this. We need new icons and rituals.

The message of Burning Man starts with modern society's desperate search for fresh bread. Many festivalgoers are former Christians bored with the static predictability of contemporary church life. Their journey into the desert is both a repudiation of religion's stale forms and a search for the supernatural magic that once attended Israel's Canaan-bound tribes. Unfortunately the Burning Man experience does not deliver where it counts. It promises originality but serves up another exotic placeholder. Instead of conveying seekers to truth, it merely abets indulgence.

In this era of Hollywood movies, high-tech theme parks and exotic novels, it is important to remember that creativity is not the ultimate tool of fantasy. Rather it is intended by God to be the ultimate interpreter of reality. As David penned in Psalm 19:1–4:

> The heavens declare the glory of God; the skies proclaim the work of his hands. Day after day they pour forth speech; night

after night they display knowledge. There is no speech or language where their voice is not heard. Their voice goes out into all the earth, their words to the ends of the world.

Just as each delicate flower and every golden sunset speaks eloquently of God's wondrous power and character, so, too, should any truly creative song or sermon. Fantasy and imagination have their place, but only to draw attention to a Master Craftsman. Apart from God they have no raw material. "The reality," Paul stated, "is found in Christ" (Colossians 2:17).

The Divine Oven

To obtain fresh bread, be it a new truth or a new wineskin, we have only to avail ourselves of the divine oven. Creativity is part of God's nature. He is forever baking new thoughts, new things and new systems.

There are, in fact, only two fundamental things we can say about God:

1. He is *uncreated.*
2. He is a *creator.*

Looking closely at these two words, we notice that one is a metaphysical fact while the other represents a moral choice. The first tells us what God is; the second, what He has chosen to do with what He is. One concerns His being; the other, His character. All His attributes can be summed up under one or the other of these fundamental aspects.[17]

God's creativity is the essence of His character. God is on the move, Guinness reminds us, and our faith should therefore manifest a certain restlessness.[18] If a message or ministry does not manifest newness, it cannot claim to have been baked in the divine oven.

SEVEN

THE FRUITFUL VINE

Knowledge may give weight, but accomplishments give lustre....

Lord Chesterfield[1]

The importance of fruitfulness is first glimpsed in God's creative pronouncements in Genesis 1. Having separated the land from the waters, the Almighty ordered the former to "bear fruit with seed in it" (verse 11) and to "produce living creatures" (verse 24). In similar fashion the waters were to "teem with living creatures" (verse 20). The resulting fish, fowl and mammals were then commanded to "be fruitful and increase in number" (verses 22, 28).

God capped this creative surge by making man and woman in His own image. As the newly minted couple opened their eyes to behold their Maker and the world He had prepared for them, God seized this profound and intimate moment to speak His first words to humanity:

God blessed them and said to them, "Be fruitful and increase in number; fill the earth and subdue it."

Genesis 1:28

Fruit is presented throughout the Bible as a symbol of life, health, blessing and accomplishment. But it does not grow wild or in isolation. Rather it is the product of trees that are watered by the river of life that flows from the heart of God.

The LORD God had planted a garden in the east, in Eden; and there he put the man he had formed. And the LORD God made all kinds of trees grow out of the ground—trees that were pleasing to the eye and good for food. In the middle of the garden were the tree of life and the tree of the knowledge of good and evil. *A river watering the garden flowed from Eden.* . . .

Genesis 2:8–10, emphasis added

Fruit trees of all kinds will grow on both banks of the river. Their leaves will not wither, nor will their fruit fail. Every month they will bear, *because the water from the sanctuary flows to them.* Their fruit will serve for food and their leaves for healing.

Ezekiel 47:12, emphasis added

Then the angel showed me *the river of the water of life, as clear as crystal, flowing from the throne of God* and of the Lamb down the middle of the great street of the city. On each side of the river stood the tree of life, bearing twelve crops of fruit, yielding its fruit every month. And the leaves of the tree are for the healing of the nations.

Revelation 22:1–2, emphasis added

When Moses sent men to explore the Promised Land of Canaan, they, too, came back with a report of this heavenly fruit:

"We went into the land to which you sent us, and it does flow with milk and honey! Here is its fruit."

Numbers 13:27

Later on God indicated His favor toward Aaron by causing his staff to bear fruit:

> The next day Moses entered the Tent of the Testimony and saw that Aaron's staff, which represented the house of Levi, had not only sprouted but had budded, blossomed and produced almonds.
>
> Numbers 17:8

The fruitful vine is God's sixth trademark, and it will be found in every life, message and ministry that enjoys His favor. This is because the Father, who "has life in himself" (John 5:26), has chosen to extend this life to those who trust Him. As Jesus said in John 10:10, "I have come that they may have life, and have it to the full."

But this abundant life is only the beginning of God's gift. He has also granted us the capacity to convey His life to others. Jesus told the Samaritan woman that His thirst-quenching water becomes in each man or woman who receives it "a spring of water welling up to eternal life" (John 4:14). And it has another powerful effect. At the same time that it quenches our thirst for love and meaning, it provokes an overwhelming hunger to serve those who remain spiritually homeless. Jesus explained to His disciples that His "food" was "to do the will of him who sent me and to finish his work" (verse 34).

> "Do you not say, 'Four months more and then the harvest'? I tell you, open your eyes and look at the fields! They are ripe for harvest. Even now the reaper draws his wages, even now he harvests the crop for eternal life, so that the sower and the reaper may be glad together."
>
> verses 35–36

Jesus said, "The words I have spoken to you are spirit and they are life" (John 6:63). Can the same be said of our own words? Or of those spoken by whatever preacher, writer, singer or recruiter is trying to gain our attention? Does the ministry that would count us among its supporters deliver true life, health and blessing—or merely religious forms and platitudes? What can it point to as godly accomplishment?

Character and Harvest

When we describe a message or ministry as being a fruitful vine, we mean that it yields results that are both measurable and consistent. But what do we mean by *results?*

In Scripture fruit can be related to either harvest (souls reached for Christ) or character (the manifestation of Christlike qualities). Examples of the former are found in Proverbs 11:30, Luke 8:5–8 and John 4:35–36, while the latter is referred to in Hosea 10:12, Galatians 6:8–9 and Ephesians 5:9.

Modern ministries have become adept at measuring harvest fruit (to the point of creating new terms, maps, programs and organizations) but are less certain when it comes to grading character. Often the two types of fruit are placed at odds. We hear about ministers who "get results" (in terms of numbers) but lack character. We are presented with sermons on "character versus results." But this is a false dichotomy. There is no need for us to choose between character and results. Indeed character *is* a result!

Paul spoke to the Colossians about "bearing fruit in every good work" (Colossians 1:10) and prayed that the Philippians might be "filled with the fruit of righteousness" (Philippians 1:11). Jesus admonished the Pharisees and Sadducees to "produce fruit in keeping with repentance" (Matthew 3:8) and encouraged His disciples to bring forth fruit that remains (see John 15:16, NKJV). David spoke of similar things in his Sabbath psalm:

> The righteous will flourish like a palm tree,
> they will grow like a cedar of Lebanon;

planted in the house of the LORD,
they will flourish in the courts of our God.
They will still bear fruit in old age,
they will stay fresh and green.

Psalm 92:12–14

In each of these cases, fruit is assumed to be the result of appropriate choices. Those who "keep in step with the Spirit" (Galatians 5:25) will find the characteristics, or fruit, of His Spirit, including

- love
- joy
- peace
- patience
- kindness
- goodness
- faithfulness
- gentleness
- self-control

manifested in their lives (see Galatians 5:22–23).

As we noted at the end of chapter 5, Christian character is never given as a gift. It is, rather, a prize that must be contended for. It is a crown reserved for overcomers, the inevitable result of godly choices. As Follette observed in *Broken Bread:*

> Righteousness is imputed to us on the basis of His redemption, but never Christian character—this is the product of training, overcoming, discipline, trial, hardship, and intensive spiritual living. . . . I cannot earn salvation, but by his grace I can *overcome* and thus become Christlike in life and character.[2]

Follette found the derivation of the word *character* to be both interesting and suggestive:

It comes from a Greek word which means to scratch, furrow, or plow. The Greek sculptors had a little instrument by the same name which they used in working upon the material before them. The instrument was a 'character,' and *charassin* was to furrow or plow or scratch. The artist worked out by plowing and furrowing the desire of his heart. So you see, our character is whatever is plowed or furrowed upon us. It is that which gives us our distinction and makes us different from others.[3]

Passages like Romans 8:29, 2 Corinthians 3:18, Ephesians 4:13 and 1 John 3:2–3 leave no doubt that the work and intent of the Spirit today is conforming, molding and shaping our lives into the likeness and image of God. He is after Christian character.

Be this as it may, godly character remains woefully undervalued in comparison to giftedness. It is still the talented speaker and the charismatic leader who command the attention of the modern Church. There is nothing wrong with a silver tongue, a keen mind or a genuine spiritual gift, but these endowments offer no guarantee that the resulting fruit will be godly. Giftedness can be acknowledged and even appreciated, but we should reserve our esteem for men and women of character. Popular speaker and *Charisma* magazine columnist Juanita Bynam observed that

> the only real proof of the presence of God in a person's life is the fruit of the Spirit. . . . [Indeed] the worst state any person can be in is to have gifts without fruit. . . . When an Old Testament priest went into the holy of holies, he tied bells and pomegranates around his waist. I believe there was a reason for that. . . . When you look at the way the pomegranates and the bells were tied around the priest's waist—one pomegranate, then one bell; one pomegranate and another bell—the bells didn't clang together unnecessarily. The fruit helped control the noise. I believe the Lord is saying the same thing to us today. Gifts without fruit are like excessive noise.[4]

Vines, Wolves and Fig Trees

Judging has lately become one of the most socially incorrect concepts in the modern Church. Many leaders are so fearful of being tagged with this label that they refuse steadfastly to condemn any attitude or behavior that Scripture does not censure emphatically. (Some are even reluctant to take a stand on more explicit prohibitions such as homosexuality, adultery and false prophecy.) Instead of siding with God against sin and mixture, these ministers have adopted the "hear-no-evil, see-no-evil" habits of many medical and police fraternities. Some hold their tongues because they live in glass houses, others because they covet access to the crowds and riches controlled by character-poor leaders.

The result of this new tolerance has been an eroded standard of holiness that has, in many cases, repelled the presence of the Holy Spirit (or at least made Him a less frequent visitor to our conferences and houses of worship). To make up for this crucial absence, Christian leaders have increasingly had to rely on mutual admiration societies and sophisticated religious programming.

As unfortunate as this situation has become, it does us no good to revert to the narrow definitions and smothering legalism of the Pharisees. Jesus never reconciled with these self-appointed guardians of orthodoxy, and there is no indication that He is prepared to do business with their contemporary descendants. Judgment that proceeds out of a proud and critical heart is religious poison. Those who engage in this behavior may think they are doing God a favor, but they are actually ripening for their own day of judgment (see Matthew 7:1–2; Romans 2:1–3; James 4:12).

Paul instructed the Corinthians to "judge nothing before the appointed time," but rather to wait for God to "expose the motives of men's hearts" (1 Corinthians 4:5). Paul understood, as did David before him, that the heart can be exceedingly difficult to read. For this reason the job of discerning its true allegiance is best left to one whose eyes can penetrate both pretense and false assumptions.

This does not mean we should accept all messages and ministries at face value. "It is required," Paul told the Corinthians, "that those who have been given a trust must prove faithful" (1 Corinthians 4:2). There are certain issues within the Church that God expects us to judge. Paul went on to explain that we "must not associate with anyone who calls himself a brother [a fellow Christian] but is sexually immoral or greedy, an idolater or a slanderer, a drunkard or a swindler. With such a man do not even eat" (1 Corinthians 5:11). When the Corinthians were waffling over the discipline of an immoral church member, the apostle wrote sternly:

> What business is it of mine to judge those outside the church? Are you not to judge those inside? . . . Do you not know that we will judge angels? How much more the things of this life!
>
> 1 Corinthians 5:12; 6:3

In similar fashion Jesus warned His disciples to "watch out for false prophets. They come to you in sheep's clothing, but *inwardly* they are ferocious wolves" (Matthew 7:15, emphasis added). Jesus' use of the word *inwardly* was indicative of a hidden motive or intent—the very kind that can be so difficult to discern accurately. But rather than tell His disciples to back off and let God "expose the motive of men's hearts," He instead explained to them how to take their own reading:

> "By their fruit you will recognize them. Do people pick grapes from thornbushes, or figs from thistles? Likewise every good tree bears good fruit, but a bad tree bears bad fruit."
>
> Matthew 7:16–18

How do we reconcile this admonition to scrutinize spiritual fruit with God's earlier injunction to judge nothing? There are two things to be said here. First, there is a difference between recognizing a condition and passing sentence on it. The former requires us to judge content (something that *is* our business), while the latter involves an assessment of guilt (something that is decidedly *not* our business). Second, God asks us to judge between fruit that is good and bad, not between fruit that is ripe and unripe. Evil is something that can and must be recognized for what it is; immaturity is a flawed shell that can sometimes obscure a good heart. Whereas the former can often be detected by trained amateurs, the latter requires an expert observer.

The spiritual yield of our lives will always fall into one of three categories:

Good fruit/life-sustaining (Psalm 1:3; Jeremiah 17:8; Galatians 5:22–23)

Bad fruit/life-destroying (Deuteronomy 32:32; Isaiah 5:2; Jeremiah 24:2; Hosea 10:1, 13; Matthew 7:17)

No fruit/lifeless (Matthew 13:22; 21:18–19; Luke 13:6–7)

While the dangers of bad fruit are obvious—Jesus associated it with wolfish or predatory motives (see Matthew 7:15)—fruitlessness is judged no less harshly (see Matthew 21:19; 25:24–30; John 15:6; Hebrews 6:8). This is because the fruitless life or ministry is one that has failed to convey the divine life to others. Since it offers no nourishment to spiritually hungry people, it serves no real purpose. Like the barren fig tree mentioned in Luke 13:6–7, it is an unprofitable parasite that leeches away valuable Kingdom resources. It offers a form of godliness but no real power. For this reason, Jesus said, "Every tree that does not produce good fruit will be cut down and thrown into the fire" (Matthew 3:10).

Good spiritual fruit comes from maintaining an organic connection with the "true vine" (John 15:1–2, 5) and remaining "planted by streams of water" (see Psalm 1:3). It is also the product of spiritual understanding (see Matthew 13:23) and the subordination of our self-interest (see John 12:24). In short, good fruit is the best—and only—evidence that a life or ministry has attained intimacy with Christ. It is a trademark well worth looking for.

Measuring Success

Spiritual fruit should be abundant as well as good. Jesus said that His Father is glorified when we "bear much fruit" (John 15:8). For the godly man or woman this poses no problem. Healthy results, whether in character or harvest, are the natural byproduct of a life or ministry animated by God's Spirit.

The only question is how we should go about measuring our success. Mistakes can lead us into deception and even divine judgment. To avoid these unpleasant consequences, we must look past

1. *Possessions* (moths and rust corrupt these—see Matthew 6:19–20)
2. *Gifts* (there is no virtue in these—see 1 Corinthians 13:2–3, 8)
3. *Accomplishments* (David was chastised for counting these—see 2 Samuel 24:2–10)

The most common of these potential stumbling blocks (accomplishments) is also the most subtle. This is because we are called to numerical success (see Luke 8:8; 19:12–19) and because accomplishments, by their very definition, are actions that must be acknowledged to have any strength or validity.

But acknowledging our accomplishments and focusing on them are two very different things. The first is a necessity, the latter an obsession. If we do not conduct periodic surveys of the spiritual battlefield, we will never know if the enemy has been defeated or if the harvest has been brought in. But if we tally and catalog our accomplishments, we risk becoming ensnared by a spirit of pride and independence.

David was a military commander who needed to know the score at the end of the day. Had Israel prevailed on the battlefield or had she suffered defeat? For a while the great warrior was content with bottom-line reports, reports he translated frequently into songs of praise:

> I pursued my enemies and crushed them;
> I did not turn back till they were destroyed.
> I crushed them completely, and they could not rise;
> They fell beneath my feet.
>
> 2 Samuel 22:38–39

On another occasion, however, David sent his military commanders out to count the troops "so that I may know how many there are" (2 Samuel 24:2). It proved an ill-fated move.

> David was conscience-stricken after he had counted the fighting men, and he said to the LORD, "I have sinned greatly in what I have done. Now, O LORD, I beg you, take away the guilt of your servant. I have done a very foolish thing."
>
> 2 Samuel 24:10

Measuring quantity alone does not tell us whether fruit is good or bad. A layer of artfully stacked fruit in a market stall can easily obscure a foundation of bruised or unripe pieces. In the same way, large, enthusiastic audiences often lead pastors and conference hosts to overlook (and sometimes ignore) mixed motives and chronic immaturity. Attention is focused on the fruit of promotion (attendance figures) rather than on the fruit of the Spirit (Christlike character).

Unripe Fruit

Church growth and church spread are often seen as prime examples of the fruitful vine. And in some cases this may be true. It all depends on whether the growth occurring inside the church(es) is having any appreciable impact on the community at large. Too often it does not. Citing the ineffectiveness of many churches, inner-city pastor John Eckhardt no longer looks "at the number of churches in an area, but the number that are having an *impact!*"[5]

Isolated church growth is largely unimpressive. There can be a hundred explanations for increased attendance, many of which are not even spiritual. (These might include a comfortable facility, conveniently scheduled services and an articulate and charismatic pastor.) Church growth is not evil, but neither is it synonymous with Kingdom growth (community transformation).

Researcher George Barna has observed that churches with a lasting impact on their communities typically measure their programs by a different statistical yardstick than their less successful counterparts. Their focus is on how many changed lives are resulting from their outreach. Barna adds:

> This differs from the experience of stagnant churches, where a program is usually evaluated according to how many people are involved as either leaders or participants. Unfortunately, while many people may be involved, the program may become simply a social clique or a safety net, rather than an effective outreach.[6]

In other cases a genuine but limited move of God is transformed into a spiritual fad or curiosity. People camp in the experience rather than use its lessons and power to impact the surrounding community. Others make pilgrimages to these visitation sites in order to bask, often vicariously, in the afterglow of God's presence. As a consequence Toronto, Pensacola, Smithton and even Willow Creek have become evangelical versions of Lourdes and Fatima.

But as Robert Stearns rightly points out, "God is after more than wells to which people can travel and be refreshed."[7] He wants to raise the spiritual tide in our own communities.

These localized and often short-lived visitations can easily become the latest fad or program. British Bible teacher Campbell McAlpine calls these "spiritual cul de sacs." We circle around, sometimes for years, until we realize we are not getting anywhere. The only exit is to recognize that the particular visitation, truth or program emphasis is not the climax but rather the starting point of God's ambitions.

Winning converts is a good thing, but unless and until they are turned into disciples, the victory is not yet ripe. In the same way church growth must mature into a more holistic expression of God's Kingdom. The Father may be pleased with new converts and growing churches, but He will not be satisfied until the entire community has been transformed. The vine He has pruned will yield grapes that are ripe, nourishing and long-lasting.

Phantom Liberations

The great nineteenth-century novelist and poet Sir Walter Scott once criticized the work of Felicia Hemans because it contained "too many flowers, too little fruit."[8] The same might be said of many of today's Christian books, conferences and ministry initiatives. Their ability to attract attention goes without question, but what are they yielding in terms of changed lives?

The problem here is not the presence of unripe fruit; it is the lack of any fruit at all. What appear to be genuine results are either phantoms or ephemeral blooms. They are, as Thomas Moore penned in his exotic poem *Lalla Rookh*,

like Dead Sea fruits, that tempt the eye,
But turn to ashes on the lips![9]

C. Peter Wagner, in his commentary on the Acts of the Apostles entitled *Spreading the Fire*, draws attention to the late Donald McGavran's call for "a theology of harvest."

McGavran is impatient with missionaries and evangelists satisfied with searching for the lost with little or no regard for how many are ultimately found. Too many Christian workers have seen such little fruit for their labors that, McGavran says, they "had to find a rationale for existence and continuance that did not depend on numbers or converts." They would say, "Results should not be used to evaluate success or failure."[10]

This is no less outrageous than a field athlete asking a meet official to lower the bar so he or she can jump over it. But there is no evidence, in Scripture or anywhere else, that God rewards such puny (translate: lazy) efforts. He will train us to jump higher but He will not lower the bar. Faithfulness is no substitute for fruitfulness. We are not called to go into all the world and be faithful; we are called to "make disciples of all nations" (Matthew 28:19).

Others recognize the need for results but are afraid or unwilling to put their lives on the line to achieve them. Instead they invent battles and box with shadows. A good example of this sanitized warfare was provided by Dr. Barry Chant, president of Tabor College in Sydney, in an article questioning the efficacy of some of today's more popular claims and practices.

Years ago, as a university student, I was involved in national service training in the army. When it came to weapon training, we were not even allowed to use blanks, for fear of igniting a fire in the tinder-dry ranges of South Australia in mid-summer.

Our platoon had to defend a hill from attack from the "enemy". We were to call out whenever we would normally have fired our weapons. I was in the mortar unit. So we sat on our rocky hill, four young students, repeatedly shouting at the tops of our voices, "Boom! Mortar!"

Below us were others crying, "Bang! Anti-tank gun!" or, "Bang! Rifle!" or, "Rat-atat-tat! Machine gun!" As the shadows lengthened, and our throats became parched, there was a momentary pause, and a solitary voice echoed out over the trees, through the still evening air—"Swish! Bow and arrow!"

It is hard to escape the impression that some of the spiritual warfare methodology being pursued today may be equally ineffective. There is a great deal of noise and bluster, but how much are we really achieving?[11]

Conjured victories are increasingly common in Christian circles. Every week some foot-stomping, cliché-chanting, perspiration-soaked crowd is commanding the prevailing powers of darkness to beat a hasty exit. Unfortunately claims of resulting "breakthroughs" are often difficult to verify. Like children playing make-believe, many prayer warriors make bold and grandiose statements because they know they will not be required to back them up. While this does not make them duplicitous or immoral, it highlights a lack of real battlefield experience. Their zeal may be praiseworthy, but their apparent fruitlessness is cause for concern.

If the evil powers at work in a city really have been "broken" (or, to use a more popular phrase, had their "assignments canceled"), are we not justified in asking why there is no supporting evidence? As I noted in *The Twilight Labyrinth:*

> To answer that the breakthrough has simply not yet been made manifest is either misguided or disingenuous. Phantom liberation is meaningless to those who remain captive to sin and death.[12]

The spiritual battlefield may include the heavenlies but it cannot exclude the earth. Unless and until deliverance becomes manifest, it is no deliverance. God is not interested in "decisions for Christ" (be they TV call-ins or raised hands at a mass crusade) if these individuals do not go on to become disciples. Nor is He interested in large churches that remain planted in social cesspools. He is after transformation, and He tallies only fruit that lasts.

Fruitful Christians are not afraid of scrutiny. In fact, they welcome it.

EIGHT

The Solid Rock

Every good and perfect gift is from above, coming down from the Father of the heavenly lights, who does not change like shifting shadows.

James 1:17

In the summer of 1990 I boarded a crowded ferry in Tangier, Morocco, and set sail for the British colony of Gibraltar. The journey across the fabled Straits separating the continents of Africa and Europe was memorable. Despite a thick orange haze that hung in the August air like an unwelcome extra blanket, it was possible to see the massive granite monolith that marks the Iberian Peninsula's southernmost tip long before we arrived. As the famous Rock loomed ever larger, I could not help but imagine the thousands of ancient and contemporary mariners that have used this landmark, also called the Pillar of Hercules, to guide their passage out of the Mediterranean into the vast Atlantic Ocean. I was also reminded of an even older Rock that has sheltered and inspired spiritual sailors for millennia.

Moses was the first to mention the Rock as he sang of God's ways before the children of Israel:

> I will proclaim the name of the LORD.
>   Oh, praise the greatness of our God!
> He is the Rock, his works are perfect,
>   and all his ways are just.
> A faithful God who does no wrong,
>   upright and just is he. . . .
> For their rock is not like our Rock,
>   as even our enemies concede.
>
> Deuteronomy 32:3–4, 31

Hannah used nearly the same words when she dedicated Samuel to the Lord:

> "There is no one holy like the LORD;
> There is no one besides you;
> There is no Rock like our God."
>
> 1 Samuel 2:2

David also sang of this Rock when the Lord delivered him from the hand of Saul:[1]

> "For who is God besides the LORD?
>   and who is the Rock except our God?
> . . . The LORD lives! Praise be to my Rock!
> Exalted be God, the Rock, my Savior!"
>
> 2 Samuel 22:32, 47

The prophet Isaiah lamented in an oracle against Damascus:

> You have forgotten God your Savior;
>   you have not remembered the Rock, your fortress.
>
> Isaiah 17:10

God's seventh and final trademark is the solid rock, an ever-present symbol of protection, provision (see Exodus 17:6; Job 29:6; Psalm 105:41) and constancy. The life or ministry that exhibits this heavenly ensign will be to the public an oasis of refreshment and a beacon of hope.

The Divine Constant

God's character is like the summer sunrise—resplendent in beauty and utterly dependable. To fully appreciate these qualities, however, one must be a consistent or long-term observer. A solitary dawn, no matter how glorious, cannot demonstrate faithfulness.

Like the massif of Gibraltar, a Kingdom-based message or ministry will endure "from generation to generation" (Daniel 4:34). It will hold steadfast against the winds and tides of change so that believers can find continuity between the past and the future. It will remain relevant while bearing the lines of eternity.

Some have suggested that the solid rock metaphor implies a defensive character, but this is misleading. Although endurance manifests an inherent resistance to change, it is not static. It is not about preserving the status quo, but about conveying that which is genuine and worthy. If a message or movement is truly of God, it will be relentless, removing those things that "can be shaken . . . so that what cannot be shaken may remain" (Hebrews 12:27).

This was the essence of Gamaliel's counsel to the Jewish Sanhedrin angered by the spread of the Gospel throughout Jerusalem. After citing two examples of short-lived, personality-based movements, the revered teacher advised his colleagues:

> "Leave these men alone! Let them go! For if their purpose or activity is of human origin, it will fail. But if it is from God, you

will not be able to stop these men; you will only find yourselves fighting against God."

Acts 5:38–39

Gamaliel understood that men cannot impede God-inspired, truth-driven ministry any more than they can prevent the sun from rising. Truth, like light and life, is a consummate escape artist; it may be restrained for a brief season, but it will always break out in the end.

Fads and Fundamentals

Faddish messages, projects and personalities have no depth or staying power. They are like meteors that light up the sky momentarily and then disappear. Since their emotional and financial energy is drawn from current events rather than from divine truths and calling, their performance tends to be even more volatile than the stock market. With no roots to sustain them, most wither and die under the heat of adversity.

Fundamental precepts, on the other hand, are the meat and potatoes of life. Drawn out of the divine oven (God's character) and served up by faithful servants, these truths have sustained healthy Kingdom growth for more than two millennia—certainly long enough to meet Gamaliel's test of authenticity.

It was this revealed truth that Jesus had in mind when He said to Peter, "On this rock I will build my church, and the gates of Hades will not overcome it" (Matthew 16:18). While Christ's early followers have long since been vindicated, the staying power of their movement has had more to do with personal relationships than with organized religion. Spiritual forms, like spiritual fads, are acutely unsatisfying and under-nourishing. Their ephemeral nature teases and disappoints like a desert mirage or a spool of cotton candy.

True faith, which the writer of Hebrews tells us "is the substance of things hoped for, the evidence of things not seen" (Hebrews 11:1, KJV), is nothing like this. The word *substance* is derived from the Greek *hupostasis,* meaning "that which stands under." It declares that *something is there,* even though its form may be difficult to recognize. According to Follette, this substance "is not the object hoped for [but] rather that which stands under and supports that object in bringing it into material manifestation."[2] Paul said much the same thing when he told the church in Rome, "Hope that is seen is no hope at all. Who hopes for what he already has?" (Romans 8:24).

Evidence is the other part of faith. As I wrote in *The God They Never Knew,*

> Many feel that because faith has to do with unseen and immaterial things, there is either no such thing as evidence or, if there is, it is irrelevant to true faith. But faith is not believing without evidence.[3]

The interplay between evidence and substance is seen clearly in the account of Peter's brief walk on water recorded in Matthew 14:25–31:

> During the fourth watch of the night Jesus went out to them, walking on the lake. When the disciples saw him walking on the lake, they were terrified. "It's a ghost," they said, and cried out in fear.
>
> But Jesus immediately said to them: "Take courage! It is I. Don't be afraid."
>
> "Lord, if it's you," Peter replied, "tell me to come to you on the water."
>
> "Come," he said.
>
> Then Peter got down out of the boat, walked on the water and came toward Jesus. But when he saw the wind, he was afraid and, beginning to sink, cried out, "Lord, save me!"
>
> Immediately Jesus reached out his hand and caught him. "You of little faith," he said, "why did you doubt?"

The episode began as Peter received evidence: Jesus bid him come. The powerful assurance that arose in his heart subsequent to the divine *come* was the substance, or *hupostasis,* that brought forth the miracle. Jesus' rebuke—"You of little faith, why did you doubt?"—refers not to Peter's honest skepticism prior to any evidence, but to his failure to persevere *after* he received a word from the Lord.[4]

Many Christians venture out on a promise when it has no application to their situations at all. They endeavor to walk on water without a divine *come* under their feet. The consequence of this presumption is often blinding confusion and emotional damage. And the matter only gets worse when these individuals take it upon themselves to beckon others onto the water. Human summons may lure people out of their boats, but they cannot generate the *hupostasis* that yields miracles.

Faith should not be a struggle. We do not need to perform mental and emotional gymnastics in order to secure it. It is, rather, a rest, a calm assurance, a support. It is a solid rock on which to plant our feet. It is why Abraham "did not waver through unbelief regarding the promise of God, but was strengthened in his faith and gave glory to God" (Romans 4:20).

C. S. Lewis once said, "Faith . . . is the art of holding onto things your reason has once accepted, in spite of your changing moods."[5] It is taking recourse in the solid Rock. It is committing ourselves with confidence to His enduring truth and unchanging character.

A. W. Tozer added that

> True faith is never found alone; it is always accompanied by expectation. The man who believes the promises of God expects to see them fulfilled. Where there is no expectation there is no faith.[6]

When we waver concerning the promise of God, it is because of fear and unbelief—conditions that derive from an uncertain foundation. The only way to remedy this situation is by cultivating intimate rapport with the One whose "Come" must undergird our every step.

Strong Foundations Take Time

The biblical record shows that many great leaders spent long seasons alone with God before being released to the ministries that eventually made them famous. Moses, David and even Jesus Himself all came to know the so-called wilderness experience. Job, Esther, Joseph and Paul also spent considerable time in preparation, albeit in markedly different ways.

Leadership development is not an easy or quick process, especially when the service to be performed is for the King of kings. It takes time to cultivate relationship and develop character. But the servant who would see his or her ministry endure will choose the road of patience and perseverance. Wisdom declares in Proverbs 8:34–35:

> Blessed is the man who listens to me,
> watching daily at my doors,
> waiting at my doorway.
> For whoever finds me finds life
> and receives favor from the LORD.

Ministry that promotes instant or formula-based success is the product of human engineering and to be avoided. Unfortunately this is not always easy. The shortcut-oriented cultures of the West have become the native habitat of those who advocate and practice foundationless faith (although none would use this term). That a region blessed with the most abundant Christian teaching in history would give rise to so many ill-prepared ministers and intercessors is a sad and cutting irony. It is also an impending tragedy.

"There are lots of nice things you can do with sand," C. S. Lewis once said, "but do not try building a house on it."[7] He had in mind Jesus' warning in Matthew 7:24–27:

> "Therefore everyone who hears these words of mine and puts them into practice is like a wise man who built his house on the rock. The rain came down, the streams rose, and the winds blew and beat against that house; yet it did not fall, because it had its foundation on the rock. But everyone who hears these words of mine and does not put them into practice is like a foolish man who built his house on sand. The rain came down, the streams rose, and the winds blew and beat against that house, and it fell with a great crash."

Given the current tendency among some Christian teachers and leaders to take the path of least resistance in their ministry planning, it behooves us to ask whether the resulting programs and messages have the necessary depth of preparation. Will they endure when the winds and rain of adversity come? Ministers who shun the wilderness experience or ignore the disciplines of daily devotions with Christ cannot be expected to lead or disciple others effectively. While salvation is instantaneous, spiritual maturity is a process of yielding our talents and rights to His Lordship. Novices have their legitimate place in the Body of Christ, but that place does not include the exercise of spiritual authority (see 1 Timothy 3:6). Disciples promoted prematurely will be asked for bread they do not have.

Temporal Vessels and Living Truth

Precious objects and heirlooms often survive a long succession of owners or custodians.[8] While this longevity is sometimes the consequence of chance or rugged construction, it is more likely the byproduct of intrinsic or perceived value. The more valuable an object is considered, the more people will cherish and care for it.

This notion of enduring value is the central theme of the 1999 motion picture *The Red Violin*. The story begins as the seventeenth-century Italian master craftsman Nicola Bussotti creates the perfect violin as a gift for his unborn son. When the artisan's wife and infant die tragically in childbirth, the instrument is launched on an epic journey. The first stop is a German orphanage, where it is picked up by a young prodigy named Kaspar Weiss. Unfortunately the boy suffers from a congenital heart defect, and collapses during his first recital. From here the violin is carried by a band of gypsies to Britain, where it becomes the prized possession of the British virtuoso Lord Frederick Pope. After the hard-living Pope commits suicide, the violin winds up in China, where it is purchased by a music teacher who tries to keep it from falling into the flames of Mao's Cultural Revolution. Eventually it makes its way to America and the hands of a shrewd appraiser's daughter.

Value, as we noted in chapter 5, obligates us. When the merchant found the pearl of great value, "he went away and sold everything he had and bought it" (Matthew 13:46). In like manner the man who discovered a treasure hidden in a field disposed of his entire estate to purchase that field (see Matthew 13:44). This man was not a land-seeker but a treasure-seeker. The field, considered alone, was of little value. It was merely a container. The treasure, of course, is God's truth and presence. And while it has been conveyed at various times in a succession of glorious containers—including a burning bush, etched tablets, the Ark of the Covenant, thundering prophets and a Child born of a virgin—these have either gone or will soon pass away. So, too, will our own earthen vessels (see 2 Corinthians 4:7).

It is the ministry or truth that endures, not necessarily the structure or the vehicle that conveys the ministry, a notable exception being Christ Himself, who "ever lives to make inter-cession" for the saints (Hebrews 7:25, NKJV). While we may loathe hearing it, our churches, agencies, programs and proj-ects are all dispensable. So are the individual vessels that organ-ize and maintain them. Commenting on this subject, the late J. Oswald Sanders said:

> It is possible to entertain an unholy solicitude for God and His work. The death of one of His workmen does not take Him by surprise and cause Him to take emergency action. Even though we may be taken unawares and shattered by the removal, we need not tremble for the ark of God. . . . No work which He has ini-tiated will be left unprovided for until His purpose through it has been achieved. . . . The fact is that no man, however gifted and devoted, is indispensable to the work of the kingdom.
>
> A shift of leadership also provides opportunity for the dis-play of the versatility of God in adapting the means to the end in view. . . . If a man possessing great gifts will not place them at the disposal of God, He [God] is not defeated. He will take a man of lesser gifts which are fully available to Him, and will supplement them with His own mighty power. . . . It is not that God does not desire to use the powers of the nobly gifted, but that few of them are as willing as was Paul to place those gifts at God's disposal.[9]

The godly man or woman will never emphasize the con-tainer over its contents, or cherish a field more than the treas-ure it contains. Nor will he or she retain a wineskin, be it a methodology or a structure, beyond its appointed time. They recognize that God's pattern of conveying truth has always been that of a relay race. Christ may be "the author and fin-isher of our faith," but in the meantime we must "run with endurance the race that is set before us" (see Hebrews 12:1–2, NKJV). In practice this means one man, one structure and one generation passing the baton of truth to another. The crown of mortal leaders does not "endure to all generations" (Proverbs 27:24, NKJV). As Sanders reminded us, "There is one Leader who holds office in perpetuity, for whom no replacement is needed."[10]

This may sound easy and logical, but few ministers can imagine how the work of God's Kingdom can continue without them or their antiquated wineskins. This spiritual dullness and the religious preservationism it engenders has become a widespread problem in today's Church. Not only does it have a stultifying effect on unity and creativity, but it tends strongly toward idolatry. For this reason it behooves us to exercise caution whenever we move into the orbit of these ministries.

The solid rock is nothing less than God's enduring truth and Kingdom. The messengers who exhibit this trademark acknowledge that they are nothing more than temporal and dispensable (if highly privileged) couriers. Convinced that the truth they are carrying will endure, they do not try to defend it. Should criticism arise, they examine it for divine revelation. If nothing comes, they continue to walk in such a way as to attract God's favor. They will quietly and humbly outlast their critics. Freed from the fatiguing task of patrolling their own kingdoms, they are able to devote themselves to the development of godly character (see 1 Peter 1:15). They come to realize, in the words of A. W. Tozer, that "among all the fancy, interest-catching toys of the world, a holy life stands apart as the only thing slated to endure."[11] It becomes one with the solid Rock.

NINE

Two Roads

In all our fallen life there is a strong gravitational pull toward complexity and away from things simple and real.

A. W. Tozer[1]

During the early 1990s reports began to surface of dramatic spiritual breakthroughs in the most unlikely places. We heard of entire communities coming to Christ in the volcanic highlands of Guatemala and the windswept reaches above the Arctic Circle. Similar accounts leaked out of the sweltering Nigerian tropics and the killing fields of Uganda, Colombia and Algeria. Of particular interest to researchers was the number of cases in which spiritual revival was followed by rapid improvements in a community's political, economic and social condition. Something was clearly going on.

In 1995 my own ministry, the Sentinel Group, began to investigate these reports in earnest. Fanning out across four continents, our researchers managed to document more than three dozen communities in the grip of this extraordinary grace. They were also able to identify many of the factors responsible for these grand testimonies. Finally, in June 1999, their discoveries were released to the public in a widely acclaimed video documentary called *Transformations*.

Revelations such as these have a way of humbling us, or at least bringing us to a point where we are willing to confront questions of genuine consequence. By lifting us to a new vantage point, they afford us the opportunity to reexamine the boundaries and meaning of our faith. The revelations provoke questions, but the right questions also lead to new revelations.

Os Guinness, one of this hour's most astute spiritual thinkers, asks one such question in his 1998 book *The Call*:

> Do we know in reality the great living truths of the faith that have a proven capacity to affect history and transform cultures as well as radically alter individual lives?[2]

Many Western Christians are unable to answer this question. Since they have never set foot in a transformed community, the very idea has a theoretical, almost mythical, cast to it. Even to discuss the subject, they must rely on imagination rather than memory.

One historian, underwhelmed by this absence of genuine spiritual experience, described Christian faith in the United States as "socially irrelevant, even if privately engaging."[3] Guinness calls this "privatized faith," a spiritual state or expression lacking in what he calls *totality*. It may be fulfilling at a personal level, but it leaves no public imprint. It has no power to transform.

Those who have *not* privatized their faith often resort to programs to compensate for their lack of experience with full-blown revival. They believe God is able to transform communities; they are just not sure His involvement can be summoned or predicted. Anxious for results, they take matters into their own hands.

Other Christians contend that while there is a place for programs, they are no substitute for the manifest presence of God. Though the former can sometimes yield impressive results, these will rarely if ever rise to the level of community transformation. In the end it comes down to line fishing versus net fishing.

This chapter will offer a thoughtful examination of these competing approaches to spiritual success—*program* and *presence*—and explain why the Western Church's infatuation with the former is hampering her ability to achieve community transformation.

The Western Infatuation with Programs

Westerners have a special affinity for programs. We like them because they are easy to start and easy to understand. They offer us a mechanism for routinizing the random, and making tangible the more abstract and unpredictable elements of our faith. Most important, they grant us a measure of control over our resources, our circumstances and even the future. What could be more comforting?

Certainly there is a place for programs. Without them many young people would never know the joys of missionary service, Gideon Bibles would never reach hotel rooms, and the refugees of war and famine would be left to fend for themselves. Programs are an integral part of God's strategy for delivering His grace to a needy world.

Like any good thing, however, programs can be abused. They can even become idols. This happens when we focus on the mechanics of an action rather than its purpose. It also occurs when we substitute our own interests for those of the Holy Spirit. Unfortunately both of these tendencies are common in Western Christendom.

Although some Christians yield to program idolatry because they have been seduced by fleshly ambition, an even greater number succumb to the sin of presumption. Having recognized a particular need or opportunity, they are filled with an irrepressible urge to *do* something. Convinced that this urge is tantamount to a divine call, they plunge headlong into activities that God has not ordained.

Such is the routine of many churches and parachurch ministries today: Identify a need and institute a program. The problem, according to noted researcher George Barna, is that "some churches fool themselves into believing that because they have a program in place, they are doing ministry. What they are really doing is *programming*."[4] God's name is on the outer skin but the core DNA is decidedly human.

Many wonder how a process that begins with such promise can end up so misguided. The answer, in many cases, is impatience. We become exercised over a given need or opportunity, and pressure God to provide us with more detail. If He fails to comply, we begin to sweat. Our prayers start to sound like a conversation between an entrepreneur and his banker or a beleaguered field commander begging for air support: *God, we're facing a critical moment. There is little time to lose. Do you copy!?* If God still does not reply, or if He fails to deliver the response we deem appropriate, our reaction is often to take matters into our own hands.

We rationalize our presumption by declaring to anyone who will listen that God *has* expressed His will. He has placed a fire in our bones that cannot be extinguished. Like Jeremiah we can no longer keep silent. We may lack critical details like project timing, the identity of partners or God's means of provision, but further revelation is just a key turn away. We only need to start the engine.

It can be exceedingly difficult to persuade an individual on a mission to slow down. This person is convinced that the world awaits him or her, and has little patience for those who would preach clarity over speed, meditation over methods, or dependence over autonomy. Many activists, left unchecked, take on messianic airs; they become driven by the mistaken belief that the growth of their churches, and even the evangelization of the world, depend largely on the success of their programs. In the process, earnest activity is substituted for genuine change.

As a whole the non-Western world is less susceptible to the lures of program culture. This immunity stems largely from the way tribal and other indigenous peoples value patience and community. They have little interest in formulas, franchises or quick fixes. They neither demand nor expect transformation on tap. While this approach may be alien to the Western mind, it has proven extremely successful. Over the last three decades, more than ninety percent of the world's transformed communities have been found in Africa, Asia or Latin America.

Spiritual Entrepreneurs: Why I Am Afraid of Them

This section is not intended as a blanket indictment of the entrepreneurial spirit. Indeed the Bible praises risk-taking and hard work that is pursued in a responsible and directed manner (see Proverbs 12:24, 27; Matthew 25:14–30). God is no friend of the indolent and envious critic whose sole business is to tear down the ideas and accomplishments of others. Proverbs 18:9 speaks of "one who is slack in his work [as] brother to one who destroys." Journalist Henry Fairlie says much the same in *The Seven Deadly Sins Today:*

> What we are unable to achieve, we will bring low. What requires talent and training and hard work, we will show can be accomplished without them.[5]

This attitude is encountered too frequently among Christian authors, radio talk show hosts and magazine reviewers.

Lacking the talent, gumption or anointing to create something on their own, they set out to dismantle the ministries of others. Their negativism is often justified in the name of "balance," although in reality they are among the Church's most narrow and Pharisaical members. They claim to be servants of God but they offend Him daily by sowing discord among brothers (see Proverbs 6:19; Romans 16:17–18). As they are unable or unwilling to see the good in others, their faultfinding becomes a way of life.

I have no desire to join such people in sabotaging the labors of godly entrepreneurs. At the same time I am disturbed by the growing evidence of greed and presumption among Christian leaders. Too many pastors and ministry executives—to say nothing of today's self-styled prophets, apostles and evangelists—are mimicking the empire-building habits of worldly materialists.

Although new churches, programs and organizations are routinely presented as the obedient outworking of divine unction, many of these ventures are more accurately classified as entrepreneurial detours taken by ministers anxious to shed the rules and oversight of others. All too often the resulting ministries become isolated fiefdoms sustained by the wealth of those who can least afford it—the chronically poor and worldly fat cats in search of moral cover.

Because these spiritual entrepreneurs are unwilling to submit their ideas and methodologies to outside scrutiny, they are forced to create pseudo-accountability in the form of loosely structured fellowships and impotent boards. Some personalities resort to self-anointing, a strange and narcissistic act that is portrayed with cinematic brilliance by actor Robert Duvall in his movie *The Apostle*. In one particular scene Duvall, who plays a wayward Southern minister, wades out into a lonely lake where he proceeds to anoint himself an apostle of Christ. There are no witnesses to this grand event, and he must rely on his own hands to bestow, and receive, divine authority.

If the contemporary lack of accountability is not disturbing enough, there is also the tendency of many Christians to equate physical results with divine approval. If a man or woman writes a bestselling book, convenes sizable crowds, builds a huge church or raises a small fortune, we are quick to conclude that he or she commands the favor of God. The evidence seems to speak for itself.

I do not deny that success has a loud and commanding voice. My worry is that we are not attentive enough to its message. We often react to what we think we hear (or *want* to hear) rather than leaning in more closely. "This is the age of the Laodiceans," A. W. Tozer observed. "The great goddess Numbers is worshipped with fervent devotion, and all things religious are brought before her for examination."[6] We judge results on the basis of volume rather than value. Most of the time we do not even notice that we are using our own measuring devices or that our calculations fail to include the variables of motive and means.

The most talked-about attributes today are size, speed and efficiency. We like people who get things done. If these spiritual entrepreneurs cut a few corners along the way, usually in the form of loosely handled truth or abused relationships—well, who hasn't? Any pain or shortcoming is quickly forgotten once the new sanctuary opens its doors or the new station goes on the air.

The argument that success is its own bottom line scares me. So do the people for whom this semantic cloak is fashioned. Too often they are ambitious, flesh-driven personalities whose accomplishments are used to conceal a spirit of independence. They may get things done, but their methods and motives are little removed from those of most self-serving politicians. They want to build a personal legacy, and they want to do it with the resources of others.

Such is the ambition of Dean Jocelin, a proud and relentlessly driven priest in William Golding's powerful novel *The*

Spire, who wants to add an elaborate pinnacle to Salisbury Cathedral. Dean Jocelin's antagonist is a cautious and seasoned master builder named Roger. The priest attempts to persuade Roger of the project's legitimacy by speaking with conviction of biblical heroes who were called by God and who then delivered the impossible. It is a powerful argument, buttressed by the force of biblical precedent and the dean's own commanding personality and position.

Golding's story is set in the fourteenth century, but the questions it raises are no less relevant today. "Was Dean Jocelin truly called? Or was he using God to countersign his own vision and energy raised to the level of hubris? God only knows," writes Guinness in his commentary. "The line is impossible for us to draw." What we do know is that the spire was eventually built and that it stands still. "The 'devouring Will' of the Dean overpowered the reluctance of the master builder and forced the project upward to its logic-defying success."[7]

Spiritual entrepreneurs, be they megachurch pastors or the heads of worldwide ministries, must first determine if they are truly called of God. And even if the answer is yes, the danger is not over, for them or for us. This, as Guinness points out, is because

> the reverse side of calling is the temptation of conceit. . . . People who are called are especially vulnerable to pride because of the very nobility of calling. Temptation is always the tempter's compliment to the tempted, so the strongest temptations are always the subtlest.[8]

Guinness calls pride "the sin of the noble mind," and laments that "chosenness and conceit have grown so close that many people confuse the two." Claims of chosenness are now regarded, cynically or astutely, as "an elegant theological fig leaf to cover self-flattery."[9]

The chief question, first asked of the celebrated poet John Milton, is this: Do we believe in God or do we believe in ourselves (and believe that God does, too)? Those fortunate enough to possess extraordinary gifts or a profound sense of calling may never learn the answer—unless or until they are truly tested.

With or without these uncertainties, the danger faced by spiritual entrepreneurs does not begin to compare with the danger they pose to others. Once again Guinness captures both the subtlety and the seriousness of the problem:

> As *The Spire* illustrates, one of the most common, subtle, and manipulative distortions of all is in religious empire building. God only knows how many churches, missionary societies, charities, colleges, crusades, reforms, and acts of philanthropic generosity have trumpeted the call of God and advanced their leaders' egos. In a generation's time this flaw will probably be seen as the single greatest problem of the megachurch movement. More than any part of the church of Christ should, today's big churches and parachurch organizations rise and fall by the strength of a single person.
>
> It is easy to abuse vision and make it serve as chaplain to our conceits or bellhop to our desires. . . . "My cause (whatever it is) is God's gift to the world," the heroic founder says in effect. "His (or her) calling (whatever it is) is God's gift to our cause," loyal followers repeat in a hundred reverent ways. So the call of God is enlisted to camouflage ego, stifle disagreement, excuse failure, decry opposition, and gild the commemorative plaques of success.[10]

Unaccountable entrepreneurs are walking time bombs. Their measure of grace, occasionally extended by concerned and passionate intercessors, can give out at any moment. The devil will also cover sin for a season in order to promote maximum damage. If there is no firewall to contain the blast, flying shrapnel will shred countless lives and entire ministries.

"Churches run toward complexity," Tozer notes in *God Tells the Man Who Cares*, "like ducks take to water." This tendency, he believes, arises out of the same motive that drove Dean Jocelin:

. . . a natural but carnal desire on the part of a gifted minority to bring the less gifted majority to heel and get them where they will not stand in the way of their soaring ambitions.[11]

Elite visionaries, now commonly referred to as apostles, are not God's only means of accomplishing His purposes in a community. Nor are they necessarily the *best*. Indeed if there is no compelling need for a stand-out leader, or if genuine accountability systems are not in place, the previously mentioned risks argue against such an arrangement. The Israelites learned this the hard way when Saul suffered his moral meltdown. God had earlier tried to persuade them to forgo an earthly king, but they refused to listen. He did this, as I noted in *The Last of the Giants,* because he knew that man-inspired initiatives turn quickly into manmade substitutes.[12]

This is not to say that God does not sometimes call talented leaders. Nor is it intended to discount the genuine and important role of apostles in the Body of Christ. My only point is that the most effective and safe leaders are those who shun the pedestal. This is certainly the case in Cali, Colombia, where a season of dramatic revival has been shepherded by a humble and largely unheralded ministerial collective. "Unity in Christ," Tozer once said, "is not something to be achieved; it is something to be recognized."[13]

Since the release of our *Transformations* video (which in its first twelve months sold more than eighty thousand copies and reached more than 120 nations), it has seemed as though churches and ministerial associations everywhere are trying to "do" unity. But I have yet to see it achieved through human effort. This is because unity, like joy, cannot be sought directly. It is a byproduct of humility (which we discussed in chapter 4). Humble people do not have problems with relationships.

To reprise Joseph Garlington's astute observation, "The thing of which we are part is greater than the part we play." We may be the best eyes, ears or voice ever created, but this means nothing if we are removed from the Body. We can be grateful for who we are, but we must also remember that we do not belong to ourselves: We are the *Body's* eyes, ears or voice. This is God's conception of membership. We become "true persons," Lewis writes, "when we have suffered ourselves to be fitted into our places."[14]

In Revelation 2 and 3 we are admonished repeatedly to "hear what the Spirit says to the churches." Note the plural suffix here. It is a reminder that God does not put all His revelatory eggs into one basket. If we wish to have a fuller understanding of God's ways and purposes, we need to expand our circle of relationships.

It is folly, of course, to suggest that large-scale projects or results are always suspect, or that God is somehow averse to growth. Scripture makes no apology for increase and abundance (see Luke 8:8; 19:12–19) so long as it does not come at the expense of character and obedience (see 1 Samuel 15:22; Matthew 7:22–23; Galatians 5:25–26). As Proverbs 27:18 reminds us, "He who tends a fig tree will eat its fruit, and he who looks after his master will be honored."

Seeker-Sensitive or Spirit-Sensitive?

The program-versus-presence debate is especially intense today among students of church growth and community-wide evangelism. On one side of this debate we find revivalists insisting that spiritual success depends on the Church's willingness to welcome God's Spirit through solemn repentance and persevering prayer. Staking out the other side of the discussion, spiritual entrepreneurs advocate more of a customer-driven approach.

In recent years it is the entrepreneurs who have carried the argument. So successful have they been, at least in the United States, that church growth is now a byword for market-oriented techniques. The emphasis has shifted from Spirit-sensitive prayer to seeker-sensitive programs.

Not everyone is happy with this change. In a meditation entitled "Seekers Sought," Os Guinness observes that while the term *seeker* is in vogue, "its use in a shallow way obscures its real importance." Too often, he complains, the appellation "is used to describe the spiritually unattached of the Western world...."

> Such seekers are rarely looking for anything in particular. Often they are drifters, not seekers, little different from the "hoppers and shoppers" who surf the media and cruise the malls of the postmodern world. Uncommitted, restless, and ever-open, they have been well-described as "conversion prone" and therefore congenitally ready to be converted and reconverted *ad nauseam*—without the conviction that would stop the dizzying spin and allow them to be at home somewhere....
>
> True seekers are different. On meeting them you feel their purpose, their energy, their integrity, their idealism, and their desire to close in on an answer. Something in life has awakened questions, has made them aware of a sense of need, has forced them to consider where they are in life.... [15]

Unfortunately the problems associated with seeker-sensitive initiatives are not limited to a faulty definition of *seeker*. They also infect a number of oft-repeated claims. A prime example is the assertion that "ministry is not about programs, it's about people." While few Christians would dispute this statement, its ring is better than its substance. It is good to deemphasize programs, but highlighting the seeker can distract us from the centrality of Christ. Our focus should be on the One who draws sinners rather than on the sinners who are drawn. If an affirmation is needed, let it be this: Ministry is not about people; it's about God drawing people.

The principal flaw in the seeker-centric model is that it leaves us to wonder how sinners should be sought. Do we draw them, or does God? Advocates of this approach give lip service to divine participation, but their initial instinct is often to take matters into their own hands. They are so desperate for results that they give place to the very thing they take pains to disavow—programs!

This is not to deny the value of well-presented ministry. As Jesus made clear in His parable of the sower, the Gospel cannot bear fruit unless it is understood by the hearer (see Matthew 13:18–23). The problem today is that efforts to ensure seeker understanding often devolve into an unhealthy preoccupation with hearer interests and appetites.

Audiences are frequently given what they want rather than what they need. The appeal is made to their emotions rather than to their understanding. They demand flashy preaching and we accommodate them. They appeal for flexible rules and abbreviated services, and we deliver that, too.

In this pragmatic age, the overriding question to be asked of any message or methodology is: Does it work? Modern-day evangelists no longer need theological polish or moral content, but they *must* be able to sell.

And sell they do. Watching some fab preachers, one wonders if they do not hone their technique in front of late-night infomercials. With colored stage lights reflecting off silk-spun suits, and their intensity jacked up to near manic levels, they offer salvation as "the deal of a lifetime."

"Ladies and gentlemen, just look at these extras! Jesus comes to *you,* eagerly waiting to save *you* from hell and give *you* heaven in return. And if that's not enough, consider His special offer to bring *you* inner peace and abundant joy. Also, for *your* comfort, He will heal *your* body, *your* finances and *your* grades. Anything *you* need is available if you will but believe.

"Best of all, you can enjoy all this at absolutely no extra cost—that's right, no extra cost. And Jesus Christ is the only One who can make your life the envy of your friends. So hurry down the aisle today while this offer lasts!"

As church growth consultant George Barna points out, "It's not hard to grow a huge congregation if all you want to do is give people a pleasing performance."[16] But what happens when we are told there is no real cost involved in spiritual conversion? What are we to think when Jesus is presented as our servant rather than our Lord? When ministers highlight all that appeals to our self-interest, is it any surprise that our thoughts center on the question *How do I come out?* Does this not render salvation itself a purely selfish concept?

This danger can surface in the most well-intentioned programs. Indeed Barna notes that some of today's fastest-growing churches are infested with self-centered parishioners.

"You have to realize," one pastor explained, "that many of these people came here in the first place because they needed help. We had ministry-minded laity who were waiting for the chance to help them. The dilemma is that this person-intensive solution becomes seductive. Once someone focuses on you, on your needs, and makes you the center of attention, it's hard to give that up."[17]

One Southern clergyman believes this problem, at least in America, is attributable to bad theology. Expanding churches are becoming not only user-friendly but user-*focused*. "I'm not disputing the likelihood that what they do in those churches they do very well," he says. "The problem is that what they're doing well is not real Christian ministry."[18]

Pastor Wayne Cordiero's New Hope Christian Fellowship offers a welcome exception to this unfortunate trend. Launched in the summer of 1995, this burgeoning Honolulu church has used a clear and loving presentation of the Gospel to attract a steady stream of visitors. More importantly it has seen a majority of these seekers transformed into faithful disciples of Christ.

Three choices have saved New Hope from the problems that afflict many of today's user-centric churches. First, the leadership has refused to adopt a narrow, narcissistic mentality. Instead of focusing member attention on the church's internal needs and programs, the pastoral staff has championed an outward-looking vision that extends to the far reaches of the Pacific Rim. When Pastor Wayne is in town, he is just as likely to be found ministering in downtown banks or municipal offices as he is in his own church building.

A second saving grace is New Hope's commitment to channel its ever-increasing membership into new church plants. Although a majority of these daughter congregations are close to home—there are approximately a dozen scattered throughout the Hawaiian archipelago—other leaders are being sent as far away as Japan and the Philippines.

Finally, the New Hope staff has refused to allow their success to engender an arrogant or elitist mentality. When certain area pastors started calling New Hope's evolving ministry "Wayne's World," Cordiero did not dismiss their comment as petty jealousy. Instead he instructed his staff to examine what they might be projecting to give rise to this charge. More recently the New Hope pastors on Oahu initiated a monthly gathering for the purpose of asking God to increase their appetite for the conditions and characteristics that attract His presence. It is this presence, they believe, that will take them beyond church growth into full-fledged community transformation.

When pastors are unconvinced of Christ's ability or willingness to "draw all men to [himself]" (John 12:32), they quickly default to people-focused programs. Their decision is often bolstered by studies "demonstrating" that most people visit church on the invitation of a friend. Impressed by these new facts, they set out to "make everyone a marketer."[19]

After observing several market-oriented, seeker-sensitive fellowships, Barna concludes:

> My perception of the growing churches was that they were on a mission. . . . They had a sense of the likely obstacles, and how they planned to respond. They were leaving as little to chance as pos-

sible. They understood that building an authentic church was going to require a tremendous amount of capital—human capital as well as financial. . . . Lacking a comprehensive plan or strategy for expansion, the odds of the pieces falling together were slim to none.[20]

While Barna cautions that successful growth has more to do with a church's responsiveness to its environment than with specific programs and structures,[21] corporate revival is barely mentioned, let alone advocated, as an effective "strategy for expansion." In the end the lost are drawn by Christian marketers whose efforts are governed by a "comprehensive plan."

As I noted earlier, this over-engineering often indicates a level of unbelief in God's sufficiency. To our subconscious mind the way of revival is untested and often delayed. Program planning, on the other hand, offers immediate gratification. John White, a one-time professor of psychiatry at the University of Manitoba, rehearses this familiar inner struggle.

When I look at a colleague at work, hardened in his sin and unbelief, it sometimes seems impossible for me to see how he could possibly become a Christian. So wide is the gap between our thinking, so self-assured and at ease does my friend seem, that my prayers die on my lips. Even God could not arouse such from darkness.

I am walking, of course, by sight rather than by faith at this point. I am believing in the visible more than in the invisible Holy Spirit. Nevertheless my dilemma is a real one. A hopelessness has descended on my soul that seems impossible to shake off. Unless . . .

Unless I could somehow get him to a meeting where. . . .
Unless I could somehow get him to read. . . .
Unless I could introduce him to. . . .

What is wrong with my reasoning? It is wrong simply because it reveals that I can only believe an invisible God will work *if I can see some visible means by which he will do so*. I can believe if my

141

friend will come to the meeting. If not I really don't see how. And this is the point at which idolatry begins.[22]

According to White,

> The essence of harlotry lies in looking to other sources for what our true bridegroom gives us freely. If we approach God in humility and righteousness, has He not promised to withhold "no good thing" (Psalm 84:11)? Does not the record of the last twenty centuries show Him stimulating revivals, reformations and awakenings apart from "any mechanical aid that we could devise"?
>
> And do we or do we not belong to Him? The question is a solemn one, for in my ears I hear querulous voices of the future pleading, "Lord, did we not organize rallies in your name and in your name bring thousands to the Exhibition Hall? Lord, did we not put on a television show that brought in thousands of dollars for your cause?[23]

From Program to Presence—and Back!

The salient question of the day is not whether programs are good or bad, but where they should be engaged on the road to spiritual success. Do we adopt them as a *response* to breakthroughs, or do we regard them as the *trigger?*

As I have shown, a high percentage of Christians today view programs as *a way to get things going.* They want to see their neighbors saved, they want their churches to grow, they want to move their communities toward transformation. Unfortunately, as White noted, they can believe their invisible God will work only if they can see some visible means by which He will do so.

At worst, evangelistic programs represent a subtle form of human initiative; at best, line fishing over net fishing. They can yield results, but these will always be limited by the ceiling of human capability. If the goal is simple *church growth* (measured by increased attendance), programs can work; but if the aim is full-blown *Kingdom growth* (measured by community transformation), then human initiatives will invariably fall short. My study of transformed communities, both historical and contemporary, has yet to turn up a single success story brought about by programs.

As the Lord told Zerubbabel more than five centuries before the birth of Christ, victory comes "not by might nor by power, but by my Spirit" (Zechariah 4:6). This formula for success has not changed in the last 2,500 years. If we truly desire to see God's Kingdom manifest in our communities, our first order of business—indeed, our sole "plan and program"—must be to attract His presence. To accomplish this, we must order a renewed commitment to humility, faith, holiness, unity and prayer.

If we allow God to remain the initiator of this process, He has promised to "[make] known to [us] the path of life" (Psalm 16:11). As His revelatory DNA enters our spiritual bloodstreams, we are transformed from program-peddlers and formula-franchisers into obedient and fruitful servants. Liberated from the bonds of presumption, we discover that "the blessing of the LORD brings wealth, and he adds no trouble to it" (Proverbs 10:22).

In short, God is calling us to abandon our attachment to programs so that He might lead us down a far more rewarding path. He is reminding us that, apart from His authorship in our lives, all our hard work and clever ideas will be in vain (see Psalm 127:1). He is entreating us to adopt His magnificent trademarks as our own.

NOTES

Chapter 1: The Need for Discernment

1. A. W. Tozer, *The Knowledge of the Holy* (New York: Harper and Row, 1961, 1975), p. 11.

2. Os Guinness, *The Call* (Nashville: Word, 1998), pp. 175, 179.

3. Elmer F. Suderman, quoted in Karl Menninger, *Whatever Became of Sin?* (New York: Hawthorn, 1973), pp. 201–2.

4. C. S. Lewis, *Surprised by Joy* (New York: Harcourt, Brace & World, 1955), p. 231.

5. George Otis Jr., *The God They Never Knew* (Grand Rapids: Mott Media, 1982), pp. 1–2.

Chapter 2: The Certain Sound

1. Tozer, *Knowledge of the Holy*, pp. 9–10, 12.

2. As an example, the word *understanding* or an equivalent is found some sixteen times in the first parable (the sower) when it is read synoptically.

3. Malcolm Muggeridge, *Jesus Rediscovered* (New York: Pyramid, 1974 [1969]), p. 47.

4. Positive responses to this type of ministry can be seen in Nineveh's wholesale acknowledgment of Jonah's warning (see Jonah 3:4–10); the Samaritan woman's acceptance of Jesus' revealing remarks (see John 4:7–29, 39); the conviction of the Pentecost converts (see Acts 2:37); and Simon's request for prayer after Peter's rebuke (see Acts 8:18–24).

5. John Eckhardt, *The Ministry Anointing of the Apostle* (Chicago: Crusaders Publications, 1993), p. 40.

6. A. W. Tozer, *God Tells the Man Who Cares* (Harrisburg, Pa.: Christian Publications, 1970), p. 37.

7. This question was first asked by my good friend Kenn Gill, who presently serves as the senior pastor at First Assembly Church in Calgary.

Chapter 3: The Open Book

1. Tom Hanks, quoted in *Interview* magazine and reproduced in "Quotable Quotes," *The Reader's Digest*, February 2000, p. 69.

2. Malcolm Muggeridge, *The Green Stick, Chronicles of Wasted Time*, Vol. I (London: Fontana/Collins, 1975 [1972]), p. 220.

3. Thomas Otway, *Venice Preserved* I.i. Listed in Bergen Evans, *Dictionary of Quotations* (New York: Avenel, 1978), p. 321.

4. C. S. Lewis, *The Lion, the Witch and the Wardrobe* (New York: Macmillan, 1950), pp. 75–76.

5. C. S. Lewis, *The Problem of Pain* (New York: Macmillan, 1962), p. 19.

6. Ibid., p. 23.

7. Susanna Centlivre, *The Artifice*, V. Listed in Evans, *Dictionary of Quotations*, p. 321.

8. Andy Butcher, "How a Porn King Found God," *Charisma*, December 1999, pp. 90–98.

9. Quoted by Adrienne Gaines, "Where Are They Now?", *Charisma*, December 1999, p. 20.

10. William Bennett, *The Book of Virtues* (New York: Simon & Schuster, 1993), p. 599.

11. Muggeridge, *Green Stick*, p. 306.

12. Tozer, *God Tells*, p. 57.

13. John White, *The Golden Cow* (Downers Grove, Ill.: InterVarsity, 1979), p. 100.

14. Muggeridge, *Green Stick*, p. 302.

15. White, *Golden Cow*, p. 105.

16. Ibid., p. 103.

17. See also 1 Chronicles 28:9; Psalm 26:2; 139:1; Proverbs 17:3.

Chapter 4: The Reflected Throne

1. C. S. Lewis, "Christianity and Literature," in *Christian Reflections*, Walter Hooper, ed. (Grand Rapids: Eerdmans, 1967), p. 6f.

2. Simple form story originally submitted by Alan Thompson of Crozet, Virginia. Reprinted in *Parables*, July 1990.

3. Quoted by Muggeridge, *Green Stick*, p. 105.

4. Tozer, *God Tells*, p. 25.

5. See also Galatians 5:26.

6. A. W. Tozer, *The Set of the Sail* (Camp Hill, Pa.: Christian Publications, 1986), p. 17.

7. Ibid.

8. Tozer, *God Tells*, p. 61.

9. Ibid., p. 84.

10. In other quarters the word simply means "good"—as in, "The worship was truly anointed this morning."

11. Tozer, *God Tells*, pp. 10–11.

12. John Wright Follette, *Arrows of Truth* (Springfield, Mo.: Gospel Publishing, 1969), p. 111. Note: According to 2 Peter 1:21, "Prophecy never had its origin in the will of man, but men spoke from God as they were carried along by the Holy Spirit."

Chapter 5: The Good Medicine

1. Lewis, *Pain*, p. 52.
2. Tozer, *God Tells*, p. 20.
3. C. S. Lewis, *Mere Christianity* (New York: Macmillan, 1975 [1943]), p. 171.
4. C. S. Lewis, *The Four Loves* (Glasgow: Collins, 1960), p. 107.
5. Lewis, *Pain*, p. 46.
6. Muggeridge adds, "This in contradistinction to power, which is a matter of numbers, of crowd scenes" (*Green Stick*, p. 299).
7. I am indebted to my sister Heather Tayloe for this story.
8. Otis, *God*, p. 36.
9. Lewis, *Pain*, p. 40.
10. Norman Vincent Peale, *The Art of Living* (New York: Abingdon-Cokesbury, 1937), p. 10.
11. Paul Vitz, *Psychology as Religion* (Grand Rapids: Eerdmans, 1977), p. 72.
12. John Wright Follette, *This Wonderful Venture Called Christian Living* (Asheville, N.C.: Follette, 1974), p. 63.
13. Lewis, *Christianity*, pp. 164–65.
14. Watchman Nee, *Love Not the World* (Fort Washington, Pa.: Christian Literature Crusade, 1968), pp. 40–41.
15. Lewis, *Christianity*, p. 174.
16. Quoted in Lewis, *Christianity*, p. 172.
17. Muggeridge, *Jesus Rediscovered*, pp. 45–46.
18. Follette, *Arrows*, p. 44.
19. Lewis, *Christianity*, p. 167.
20. John Wright Follette, *Broken Bread* (Springfield, Mo.: Gospel Publishing, 1957), p. 183.
21. Fénelon, François de Salignac de La Mothe, *Christian Perfection* (New York: Harper & Row, 1947), pp. 83–84.
22. Ivor Griffith, quoted in *Intouch* (newsletter produced by YWAM Associates International), November 1999.

Chapter 6: The Fresh Bread

1. Tozer, *God Tells*, p. 40.
2. Lewis Carroll, "The Walrus and the Carpenter," *Through the Looking Glass*, IV, 1872.
3. Tozer, *God Tells*, p. 68.
4. Quoted in *Distilled Wisdom*, Alfred Armand Montapert, ed. (Englewood Cliffs, N.J.: Prentice-Hall, 1964), p. 41.
5. For many Christians the Sunday morning routine is summed up in the AWFULL acronym: Arrive; Worship; Fellowship; Usher; Listen; Leave!
6. Tozer, *God Tells*, p. 12.
7. Henry Miller, *Tropic of Cancer* (New York: Signet/Penguin, 1995), p. 84.
8. Guinness, *Call*, p. 107.
9. See C. S. Lewis, "Christianity and Literature," in *Christian Reflections*, pp. 6f.
10. Vitz, *Psychology as Religion*, p. 63.

11. Ibid., p. 102.

12. Ibid., p. 64.

13. J. Oswald Sanders, *Spiritual Leadership* (London: Lakeland, 1967), p. 89.

14. Quoted in Guinness, *Call*, p. 179.

15. A. A. Milne, "The King's Breakfast," *When We Were Very Young*, 1924.

16. J. G. Saxe, "My Familliar," *Anthology of American Poetry*, ed. George Gesner (Roanoke, Virginia: Avenel Books, 1983). Or there is Jonathan Swift's declaration in "On the Death of Dr. Swift": *Faith! he must make his stories shorter / Or change his comrades once a quarter.*

17. See Otis, *God*, p. 27.

18. Guinness, *Call*, p. 186.

Chapter 7: The Fruitful Vine

1. Lord Chesterfield (Philip Dormer Stanhope, 4th Earl of Chesterfield, 1694–1773), *Maxims*, in *Letters to His Son* (Third ed., 1774), Vol. 4, p. 304.

2. Follette, *Bread*, pp. 193–94.

3. Follette, *Arrows*, p. 106.

4. Juanita Bynam, "Name That Fruit!" *Charisma*, December 1999, p. 100.

5. Eckhardt, *Ministry Anointing*, p. 30.

6. George Barna, *User Friendly Churches* (Ventura, Calif.: Regal, 1991), p. 46.

7. Robert Stearns, *Prepare the Way* (Lake Mary, Fla.: Creation House, 1999), p. 138.

8. Sir Walter Scott, letter to Joanna Baillie, July 18, 1823, in *Letters of Sir Walter Scott* (Centenary Ed.), Vol. 8., ed. H.J.C. Grierson (London: Contable and Company, 1937).

9. Thomas Moore, *Lalla Rookh* (1817), "The Fire-Worshippers," Part 3, l. 356.

10. C. Peter Wagner, *Spreading the Fire* (Ventura. Calif.: Regal, 1994), pp. 82–83.

11. Cited in George K. Otis Jr., *The Twilight Labyrinth* (Grand Rapids: Chosen, 1998), pp. 277–78.

12. Otis, *Labyrinth*, p. 279.

Chapter 8: The Solid Rock

1. See also Psalm 18:2; 31:3; 40:2; 42:9; 62:2, 7; 71:3; 94:22; 95:1.

2. Follette, *Broken Bread*, p. 136.

3. Otis, *God*, p. 153.

4. Ibid., pp. 155–156.

5. Lewis, *Christianity*, p. 123.

6. Tozer, *God Tells*, p. 135.

7. Lewis, *Christianity*, p. 163.

8. In Western cultures these transgenerational treasures typically consist of family photos, valuable jewelry or a special piece of artwork. In traditional or animistic societies they are more likely to be idols, totems or medicine bundles.

9. Sanders, *Leadership*, pp. 132–3, 135.

10. Ibid., p. 136.

11. Tozer, *Sail*, p. 16.

Chapter 9: Two Roads

1. Tozer, *God Tells,* p. 32.
2. Guinness, *Call,* p. 59.
3. Ibid., p. 166.
4. Barna, *Churches,* p. 42.
5. Henry Fairlie, quoted in Guinness, *Call,* p. 129.
6. Tozer, *Sail,* p. 153.
7. Guinness, *Call,* p. 117.
8. Ibid., pp. 117, 121.
9. Ibid., p. 118.
10. Ibid., pp. 120–21, 187.
11. Tozer, *God Tells,* p. 32.
12. George Otis Jr., *The Last of the Giants* (Grand Rapids: Chosen Books, 1991), p. 89.
13. Tozer, *God Tells,* p. 49.
14. C. S. Lewis, *Fern-Seed and Elephants and Other Essays on Christianity* (London: Fontana/Collins, 1975), p. 23.
15. Guinness, *Call,* p. 10.
16. Barna, *Churches,* p. 25.
17. Ibid., p. 47.
18. Ibid., p. 63.
19. Ibid., pp. 97–98.
20. Ibid., p. 186.
21. Ibid., p. 190.
22. White, *Golden Cow,* pp. 150–51.
23. Ibid., pp. 152–53.

INDEX

abstraction, hiding in, 32–34
accountability, 18, 44–46. *See also* anointing
adultery, 105
agendas, hidden, 42, 47–48
Anderson, Ann Kiemel, 46
    Seduced by Success, 46
anointing, 62–64
appearance as reality, 41–42
arrogance. *See* teachers: false
Artifice, The (Centlivre), 44
authenticity, power of divine, 37–38
authority:
    claimed spiritual, 18
    despised, 18
    manifested, 34–38

Barna, George, 110, 129, 139, 140–41
Bennett, William, 47
Book of Virtues, The (Bennett), 47
brands, 13-15
    purposes of, 14
    See also trademark
Bread of heaven, 84
breakthroughs, spiritual, 126–27
Broken Bread (Follette), 75, 103–4
Burning Man, The, 96–97
Bynam, Juanita, 104

Call, The (Guinness), 127
Camus, Albert, 73
Carroll, Lewis, 84
celebration, true, 87

Centlivre, Susanna, 44
    The Artifice, 44
Chant, Barry, 112–13
character:
    Christian, 103
    compared with giftedness, 104
    godly, 104
    grading, 102
    spin, 44
Charisma magazine, 104
Chesterfield, Lord Philip Dormer Stanhope, 99
Chronicles of Wasted Time (Muggeridge), 42
communication:
    authoritative, 35
    focus and specificity of, 28–32
    interpretive, 35
    means of, 31
    spiritual, 27–28
communion, deep, 24
converts, 111. *See also* disciples
Cordiero, Wayne, 139–40
counterfeit items, 15
    and the spiritual arena, 15–16, 22
creativity, 84, 88–92
    and communication, 93
    and God's nature, 98
    and reality, 97–98
    and structures, 94–95

Dawson, Joy, 80–81
deliverance via abstinence, 72
discernment, 15, 106

failed, 20
of God's voice, 22–24
improvement of, 28
unconscious, 27–28
disciples, 111, 114. *See also* fruit
discipline, 38–39
discovery of God, 30–31
doctrine, unsound, 66
Duvall, Robert, 131
The Apostle (movie), 131

Eckhardt, John, 110, 34
Eldred, Ken, 54
endurance, 117
of ministry of truth, 123–24
entertainment, 90–91
entrepreneurs:
attributes of, 132
and customer-driven approach,
136–42
and elite visionaries, 135
and empire-building, 131
and God's call, 133
and pseudo-accountability, 131–32
and results, 132
and self-anointing, 131
spiritual, 130-36
episorcuo, 20–21
equivocators, 48
evil, 107. *See also* sin
exaggerators, 48

Fairlie, Henry, 130
The Seven Deadly Sins Today, 130
faith:
and fruitfulness, 112
privatized, 127
feelings, 29–32
fellowship, superficial, 33
Fénelon, Francois, 76
Follette, John Wright, 63, 71, 74, 75,
103–4
Broken Bread, 75, 103–4
fruit, and conjured victories, 113

Garlington, Joseph, 61–62, 135–36
generics, 15
and the spiritual arena, 15–16, 22

God Tells the Man Who Cares (Tozer),
66, 134
God They Never Knew, The (George
Otis Jr.), 69, 119
Golding, William, 132–33
The Spire, 132–33, 134–35
good, 108
measuring, 102, 110
of promotion, 110
of the Spirit, 103, 110
throughout the Bible, 100–101
unripe, 110–11, 112
See also spiritual yield
Green Stick, The (Muggeridge), 47
growth:
church, 140, 142–43
Kingdom, 143
Guinness, Os, 12, 88, 98, 127,
133–34, 137
The Call, 127

Hanks, Tom, 41
Hastings, Jeff, 86–87
Hemans, Felicia, 111
Hitler, Adolf, 39
holiness:
eroded standard of, 105
and legalism, 79
homosexuality, 105
honesty and suspended judgment,
41–42
See also trademark: of the open book
human greatness, measurement of,
56–57
Humbard, Rex, 86
humility, 57, 61, 64, 135
hunger of the soul, 83–84
hupostasis, 120

immortality, 23–24
impact, Christian, 110–11
integrity, 42–43
intimacy with Christ, 108
intimidation, 91–92
itching ears, 20–22

Jesus Rediscovered (Muggeridge), 74
judging, 79, 105–8
concerns about, 54

and holiness, 105
and homosexuality, 105
as religious poison, 105
spiritual fruit, 107

Knowledge of the Holy, The (Tozer),
29–30

Lalla Rookh (Moore), 112
Lane, Steve, 45–46
Last of the Giants, The (George Otis
Jr.), 135
leadership, development of, 121–22
Lear, Bill, 80–81
Lear, Moira, 80–81
Lewis, C. S.:
  and the body of Christ, 136
  and creativity, 88, 91
  and faith, 120
  and the flesh, 70
  and God, 65
  and honesty, 43
  and love, 67, 68–69
  and reflected throne, 52
  and relationships, 23–24, 72–73, 75
  and strong foundations, 122
  *The Lion, the Witch and the
  Wardrobe*, 43
  Mere Christianity, 67
  The Problem of Pain, 70
logos, 13–15
love:
  constraining, 67–70
  speaking in, 81

MacDonald, George, 74
manipulation, 49–51, 92
  religious, 16
Mao Zedong, 39
McAlpine, Campbell, 38, 111
McGavran, Donald, 112
Mere Christianity (Lewis), 67
message:
  and ambiguity, 29
  the faddish, 118–21
  Kingdom-based, 117
  See also ministry
Miller, Henry, 86
  Tropic of Cancer, 86

Milne, A. A., 92
  When We Were Very Young, 92
Milton, John, 133–34
ministry:
  approach, 57
  of bad medicine, 78
  creative, 91–92
  and deflecting attention, 59
  and entropy, 93–94
  fleshly, 70–72
  and intimidation, 91–92
  message, 58
  messenger-centric, 58–59
  self-interested, 78
  See also manipulation
Moore, Thomas, 112
  Lalla Rookh, 112
Muggeridge, Malcolm, 32, 42, 47, 49,
  68, 74
  Chronicles of Wasted Time, 42
  The Green Stick, 47
  Jesus Rediscovered, 74

narcissism. *See* peacock-ism
Nee, Watchman, 72
negligent healers, 76–81
Nietzsche, Friedrich Wilhelm, 85

obedience, 32, 64
Otis, George, Jr., 69, 113–14, 119,
  135
  The God They Never Knew, 69, 119
  The Last of the Giants, 135
  The Twilight Labyrinth, 113–14
Otis, George, Sr., 80–81

Pascal, Blaise, 54
peacock-ism, 53–56
Peale, Norman Vincent, 70
Petrie, Alistair, 52
pleasure. *See* teachers: false
pornography. *See* accountability; sin:
  secret
prayer, spirit-sensitive, 137
preaching, 92–93
  theoretical, 33
precepts, fundamental, 118–21
prescription:
  false, 22
  one-revelation-fits-all, 16

presence, 142–43
presumptuousness. *See* teachers: false
pride, 133
private ambitions, 51. *See also* sin:
  secret
Problem of Pain, The (Lewis), 70
programs:
  abused, 128
  avoiding problems with, 139–40
  evangelistic, 142
  idolatry of, 128–29
  and problems of, 137–39
  seeker-sensitive, 136–42
  Western infatuation with, 128–30
prophets, false, 16, 76–81. *See also*
  teachers: false
Psychology as Religion (Vitz), 88–89
publishers, Christian. *See* peacock-ism

reality:
  addressed by God, 33–34
  modification, 48

Red Violin, The (movie), 123
results, 102–4. *See also* character;
  disciples; fruit
routines, 84–88
Ruibal, Ruth, 81–82

sanctuary, dual meaning of, 32
Sanders, J. Oswald, 91, 124–25
Saxe, J. G., 93
Scott, Sir Walter, 111
Seduced by Success (Anderson), 46
seduction. *See* teachers: false
self-adulation. *See* peacock-ism
sense organs, spiritual, 22–23
Sentinel Group, the, 126–27
servants, see-through, 60–62
Set of the Sail, The (Tozer), 56
Seven Deadly Sins Today, The (Fairlie),
  130
sin:
  minimized, 79
  not exposed, 78
  of presumption, 129
  secret, 44–46, 51
  whitewashing of, 80–81
slippery facts, 48–49

Solzhenitsyn, Alexander, 91
speech:
  authority of, 28
  and our obligation, 32
  specificity of, 28
  See also trademark: of the certain
    sound
Spire, The (Golding), 132–33, 134–35
spiritual:
  malpractice, 16
  maturity, 122
  spiritual yield, 107
  See also fruit
Spreading the Fire (Wagner), 112
Stearns, Robert, 111
stranger, 23
  and foreigner, 23
stumbling blocks, 108–10
substance, 119
  and evidence, 119–20
success, measuring, 108–10

teachers:
  dangerous, 19–20
  and exploitation, 18, 49
  false, 17, 18–19
  heaping, 20–21
  and secrets, 17
  side-door, 17–20, 66
techniques, market-oriented, 137,
  140–41. *See also* programs: seeker-
  sensitive
theology, abstract, 33
Tozer, A. W.:
  and anointing, 63
  and churches, 85–86, 134–35
  and communication, 29–30
  and discernment, 11
  and faith, 120
  and hidden agendas, 47
  and holiness, 125, 126, 132, 135
  and human vanity, 62
  and humility, 56
  and peacock-ism, 54
  and preachers, 57–58
  and trademarks, 39
  and the world, 66, 83
  God Tells the Man Who Cares, 66,
    134–35

The Knowledge of the Holy, 29–30
The Set of the Sail, 56
trademark, 13–15
  of the certain sound, 26–40
  of fresh bread, 83–98
  of fruitfulness, 99–114
  of good medicine, 65–82
  of the open book, 41–51
  purposes of, 14–15
  of the reflected throne, 52–64
  of the solid rock, 115–25
  of the two roads, 126–43
traffic signals, divine, 24–25
Transformations (video), 127, 135. *See
  also* Sentinel Group, the
treasure, 123
Tropic of Cancer (Miller), 86
truth:
  dismissed, 79
  speaking in, 81

Twilight Labyrinth, The (George Otis
  Jr.), 113–14

value, 123
Vitz, Paul, 70, 88–89
  Psychology as Religion, 88–89
voice, learning God's. *See* trademark:
  of the certain sound

Wagner, C. Peter, 112
  Spreading the Fire, 112
wandering, 81–82
waterless wells. *See* teachers: false
When We Were Very Young (Milne), 92
White, John, 47–48, 49, 50, 141–42
windbags, 92–95
wineskins, 92–95, 124
wooing of the Holy Spirit, 49–51
Word of the Lord, 28–29

George Otis Jr. is the founder and president of The Sentinel Group, a Seattle-based Christian research and information agency whose purpose is to help Christians sustain prayer campaigns that result in evangelistic breakthroughs and community transformation worldwide.

Mr. Otis formally served as a senior associate with the Lausanne Committee for World Evangelization (Restricted-Access World) and, until recently, as the co-coordinator of the United Prayer Track of the A.D. 2000 & Beyond Movement. He is an international advisor to Aglow International and Lydia Prayer Fellowship. He is a frequent speaker at churches, schools and conferences, a role that afforded him the privilege of delivering plenary addresses at the 1989 Congress for World Evangelization in Manila, the 1990 Urbana missions conference, the GCOWE II conference in Seoul, Korea, and many other international events.

He is the author of six books, including *The Last of the Giants, The Twilight Labyrinth, Informed Intercession* and *God's Trademarks.* Mr. Otis also produced the video documentary *Transformations,* which won the 2000 Angel Award for Best Video. He is a regular guest on Christian radio and television programs, including "The 700 Club" and "Point of View." He has been featured in numerous Christian magazines and has been consulted by and/or has presented material to *The Los Angeles Times, Esquire* magazine, *Time* magazine and National Public Radio's "All Things Considered."

Mr. Otis has traveled and ministered in nearly one hundred nations, and currently lives in Lynnwood, Washington, with his wife, Lisa, and their four children.

UNLOCKING THE WORLD

For the latest resources and ministry
updates from George Otis Jr. and
The Sentinel Group, visit our
web site at www.sentinelgroup.org
or call toll-free for a
complete product catalog
at 1-800-668-5657.

Learn more about:

Community Transformation Resources

20/20 Prayer Support Program

World InSight Magazine

Ancient Pathways Project